YOU CAN TEACH YOUR
CHILD TO READ

Adrienne Katz

· ·

YOU CAN TEACH YOUR CHILD TO READ

Thorsons

An Imprint of HarperCollins*Publishers*

For Ian and Liane

Thorsons
An Imprint of HarperCollins*Publishers*
77-85 Fulham Palace Road,
Hammersmith, London W6 8JB
1160 Battery Street,
San Francisco, California 94111-1213

First published by Thorsons 1989
This edition 1993
1 3 5 7 9 10 8 6 4 2

Adrienne Katz assert the moral right to
be identified as the author of this work

Illustrations by Marcus Byron

A catalogue record for this book
is available from the British Library

ISBN 0 7225 2819 1

Phototypeset by Harper Phototypesetters Limited,
Northampton, England
Printed in Great Britain by
HarperCollinsManufacturing Glasgow

Contents

· · · · ·

Acknowledgements
· · · · ·

My thanks to Mary Caven, staff, children and parents of Prior Weston Primary School, Ceri Rowlands and Tracey Kenyon, who have a special interest in reading. To Jane Lawrence and staff at Sheen Mount Primary School, thank you for the opportunities in Miss Searle's class, and with Mrs Stanton and Mrs Goodier. I appreciate the help of the many parents and teachers who have been so generous with their time and experiences. To all the children who shared their reading with me, how are you getting on? Thank you for reading with me and for telling me so much about books.

NOTE

It is an age-old problem whether to use he or she when talking about the child. To repeat both each and every time is clumsy. To always refer to 'him' is unfair and irritating to the girls. I hope you will be understanding about the changing gender of the child from chapter to chapter.

INTRODUCTION
· · · · ·
A Love of Books

The message of this book is simple. Books make readers. Without motivation, no amount of teaching, drilling or threats can make a real reader. I want to pass on a love of books to children.

Parents may worry about their child's reading for several reasons. They worry that their child may end up among the 13 per cent of the adult population who admit to having difficulties with basic skills. As their children spend more and more time on television and video games, parents wonder what happened to reading. So many children stop reading once they have learned the skill. They are rushing off to the exciting after-school activities their friends are trying . . . football, music, ballet, tennis or pottery. Then there is the child of school age who has not broken through to independent reading, and there comes a realization that friends and classmates can read. Coping in class becomes more and more difficult as she is given more of what she cannot do and likes it less and less. A child who perceives herself as stupid and is thought by others to be so, is caught in a self-fulfilling prophecy. Reading is one of the first areas of life in which a child realizes she can fail.

Parents can help. They can give the new reader the confidence and the belief that she *can* do it. Learning to read by sharing books with a loving adult takes advantage of the child's natural learning habit. After all, we teach children to talk and to ride a bike in this way. Teaching them how to read can be just as easy.

If you are a book person yourself, you will know what books have given you over the years and you will want your children to share this. If you have not discovered the richer quality of life and thought that literature offers, you could begin to find out now, together with your child.

You and your child will be starting on an adventure that should last for years because you both enjoy it. There is nothing mysterious about learning to read. Think of reading as part of acquiring language along with talking and writing.

The environment we parents create at home, and our attitudes to learning, strongly influence our children's motivation. If possible, parents should introduce the enchantment of books when their children are babies, but if you did not start early and your child is approaching school, start now and don't worry!

Meeting the written word and finding out its meaning can be exciting and rewarding. Instead, it is often accompanied by tension, failure or simply boredom. Reading as a chore is boring. No adult would want to read a boring book, so why do we ask this of new readers? When asked, many say 'Reading is boring'. Perhaps what they're being offered to read *is* boring compared to being active. *What* is read is absolutely vital. Good content can teach because it answers the question 'Why should I read?' When you can't wait to turn the page to find out what will happen next, both you and your child will know *why* you read.

The ideas in this book emphasize the natural way in which parents can help their children to read. I hope no suggestion leads to tension or nagging on the part of the adult, for then the point will have been lost. Games and projects are for fun. Play them when your child feels like it and for as long as they are enjoyed, but if your intention is to drill your child, no game can conceal it. A good story or a book about the child's current interest will do more for both of you.

We often see reading as a start of a child's education, but actually the first step is taken by most children fairly automatically when they learn to talk. Reading is part of the acquisition of language – sounds simply have visual symbols to represent them. It is one facet of the complex use of words that the child is already on the way to mastering. By the age of 5, a chid may have a vocabulary of roughly 2,000 words. Learning to use words as tools for dialogue is the vital first step.

Teaching children to read is simpler if you remember that learning to talk was achieved in a happy, relaxed way without drills, exercises, tension or expectation of failure. You taught them by example and repetition. You were excited and appreciative when they tried to say a word. You can teach them to read in the same way.

Reading is the key to gaining knowledge. It is clear then that reading, along with writing, talking and listening, should be integrated with every aspect of our lives, not seen as a separate skill. We need it to function well. If we are to share knowledge, question and answer, gain insights and experiences, indeed to develop thought, we need to be able to use language, both spoken and written. The two are tightly interwoven. Talk to your child and listen to her, you are helping her to use and master the language she needs. Before she reads, she will need to be speaking well.

WHAT CHILDREN WANT FROM READING

It is not enough to produce a reader who, when prodded, or to please an adult, will adequately read a page from a 'reader', sometimes without making sense of it. We want our children to read with understanding. They will have to cope equally well with instruction manuals, reference books and enjoy fascinating stories.

We need to introduce children to reading in a wide sense. Schooldays are a small portion of a person's lifetime and our children can look forward to many years of enjoying books as companions, entertainment, sources of information and a well-spring of ideas and experience. We have a long-term goal over and above the immediate one of ensuring that they can read.

For a child to get the most out of reading, we need to instil a love of books. But for a child to read at all, she needs to want to. Before she can read her parents can offer a glimpse of the treasures that await her. Through books we find enchantment, sympathy, excitement, emotional sensitivity, and new experiences as well as our cultural heritage. We can consciously make the child a partner in reading. We can share books both when she is very young and as she develops and matures.

We have an influence on her motivation and attitudes, whether we are aware of it or not. If we are seen to read, and have books all around us at home, the child expects books to be part of her world. If we take obvious pleasure in books it is infectious.

In school a child is one of many - at home she is unique. This 'specialness' of a child to her parent can help to develop her talking, reading and writing. A child who lacks this rich dialogue with an interested adult is poor in spirit as well as vocabulary. We can become more aware of the power we have to make a positive contribution to a child's outlook, both consciously and by example.

If we invest in this special dialogue with a child it proves a vital and lasting bond. Our responsibility is to make sure that we do not turn a child off reading, by surrounding it with tensions or by making it seem difficult. We are not there to interpret reading as work, but to open the door to this 'life-long intoxication'.

1

. . . . .

Why Parents?

HOME IS WHERE THE HELP IS

Children who have good parental support and help learn and progress better than those who do not. Many studies prove that parents taking an interest, helping and encouraging a child on a one-to-one basis have an incalculable effect.

I will try to show how parents (or an interested carer) are uniquely suited to help their children become real readers of real books. Before your heart sinks at the thought of yet another responsibility, glance through this list of fears and worries other parents expressed at first.

Questions Parents Ask

- Do I really want to be my child's teacher? Why should this be necessary when school exists for this function?
- Will this be one mor area of parenting that might increase my sense of guilt if I don't measure up?
- How do I overcome my lack of confidence?
- How will I get the time? Will I manage to fit it into my already frantic schedule?
- I already help my child with schoolwork. If I work with him on reading, will I be thought 'interfering'?
- My child can already read. Do I need to stay involved?

- Does there have to be a problem with my child's reading before I step in?
- Does asking parents to help mean the school cannot cope?
- I have very little patience, how can I develop a listening skill?

The remarks they made some weeks later were so different: fears were unfounded, their enthusiasm for the experience and their children's enthusiasm for books was dramatic proof that parent power is a vital key to learning to read.

Parents worry too about the difference between the way they were taught and today's methods. Many schools are adopting an approach which involves parents in reading programmes as they recognize the value of home/school co-operation. This does not mean that they cannot cope or that your child necessarily has a problem. It represents current thinking.

There have been phases during which teachers advised parents *not* to teach their children to read, but now most are convinced of the importance of 'parent power'. Understandably, parents are worried about being branded 'pushy', though equally some parents may be criticized as 'not being supportive enough'. Is there a happy medium?

There is an easy way out of this minefield of anxieties. I am not going to suggest that you become a teacher, or use any sophisticated methods. Nor that you take over the responsibility of the school or monitor your child's progress like a taskmaster.

The idea is that you and your child should have *more fun and shared enjoyment*, not less. This approach offers you both an encounter with the world of literature and some 'quality time' together.

If sharing the enjoyment of books rather than 'teaching', 'testing' or checking your child's progress, can become part of your lives, you will have found the happy medium. You will need to make time for regular book adventures with your child, and to find out about established and new children's books of quality. Striking the right note with your child's teacher in order to form a good understanding is also important. These vital ingredients are dealt with in later chapters, but first take a look at the reasons why parents have this remarkable influence.

WHY PARENTS HAVE A SPECIAL INFLUENCE

Parent power is effective because education does not suddenly begin at school age. Nor does learning take place strictly within school hours and then stop. The out-of-school and pre-school experiences of a child are just as valuable.

Reading is part of language. The use that is made of language, and your child's exposure to this, has a bearing on what he learns and knows. It opens the way for reasoning, communicating and understanding. Parents, whether consciously or not, create a background, of which the child sees himself a part. His motivation and attitudes are strongly affected by this background, rather like the way in which you notice teenagers being so obviously influenced by their peer group and the fads of the time.

When a child joins 'the club of spoken word users' – as reading expert Frank Smith describes it in *Joining the Literary Club** – he is welcomed as a junior member. He is helped and encouraged, participates in club activities, and learns from what other people do, provided they are the kind of people the child sees himself as being.

Children do not learn to talk through formal instruction or special courses but progress as they join in the communication process they find all around them. This starts when they utter their first sounds and words. Every effort they make is greeted with enthusiasm. Their words are delightedly repeated by adults with much eye contact and smiling. There is no question of failure if they have not said the word perfectly. We are eager to guess what they mean and encourage them to try. In this way they learn to talk effortlessly, picking up subtle points about communicating

*Centre for Teaching and Reading & Abel Press, Victoria, British Columbia, available from the University of Reading.

along the way. They copy our facial expressions, intonation and phrasing, they use idioms and gestures and learn how to select the appropriate one of many hundreds of these. On average, infants learn at a rate of over 20 words a day.

Your baby watches you talking to others as well as to him. He is eager to join in and make you understand him. Expressions of love, lullabies and greetings surround the small baby. Gradually he identifies them and responds.

Parents could have the same influence on children's reading. Few children see their teacher absorbed in a novel during the busy school day, unless they are lucky enough to have a teacher who sets aside time for everyone to do some silent reading, and reads herself. At home your child *will* see you reading recipes, instructions for making something, train timetables, telephone directories and TV guides, as well as books and stories. When your child sits entranced as you read a story together, he knows there is ample reward for finding meaning from print.

WHY ARE PARENTS ESPECIALLY SUITED?

We need to communicate. Childcare is rewarding, exhausting and often tedious. There we are, stuck with a companion whose conversation is restricted, whose view of the world is limited and whose needs we want desperately to fulfil.

The child cries and we do not know why. This is worrying and frustrating. The sooner we teach this child to communicate the easier it will be. So there is a natural drive in most parents to get through to their baby on many levels. Dialogue will develop as we learn to interpret the baby's sounds and he studies our sounds in response.

There is as much satisfaction for adult as for baby when a need is met, when the request was understood and fulfilled. So, from the start both sides have an urge to communicate, and feel pleased when dialogue is established. This pleasure is increased as our offspring learn to talk in an astoundingly rapid feat of learning.

When we respond with delight we look into our baby's eyes, we smile, perhaps cuddle. We often repeat the word and a loving glow envelops us both. *We have in fact taught that child that communicating is rewarding.*

We could extend this to reading and writing now that we know that *security, warmth and affection are more powerful than any special techniques.* We can read to and with the child as we spoke to and with him while he was learning to talk. We can use writing alongside talking and reading. There are many other reasons why we have a special parental contribution to make to our child's learning.

PARENT'S CONTRIBUTION

- Parents can give a child a few minutes of *undivided attention.* To us this child is unique, special and loved. Sharing a book with him is one more way of letting him know this.
- Even the warmest teacher cannot have this important one-to-one relationship with your child. Busy teachers may not spend more than a few minutes hearing your child read in a day. Researchers have found that some manage as much as 10 or 15, most average two or three minutes.*
- Parents are there year after year! Teachers change. Our attitude to language and books will be a lasting influence.
- As parents, you have the advantage of being able to *pick the moment* or, rather, letting your child pick the moment he would like to share a book with you. You can let this activity take as much or as little time as the child would like.
- You can show a child that *books equal pleasure.* Enjoying books together, cuddling and laughing together, creates a close physical and emotional experience for the child.
- You can turn *books into friends.* Your child learns in an unhurried way that you can return again and again to a loved book. At

*W. Southgate, *Extending Beginning Reading,* Heinemann, 1981.

home there is no need to progress to the next colour-coded group of books, on the very day he wants to be comforted by an old favourite. (Watch how even fluent 8- and 9-year-old readers suddenly re-read a babyhood book lovingly to dollies or teddy bears.)

- It is *easier* for a parent to encourage and delight a child in the early years, than to settle into a pattern of urging and nagging a reluctant reader later.
- Parents represent the culture and background of the family and its linguistic roots. 'The bones of my people are in my words.'
- Remedial teachers believe that the earlier a child is helped over a problem, the better the result. Parents are often the first to realize that the child may need professional help with learning to read in those few cases where there is some serious difficulty. Close involvement with the child will reveal any difficulties to the parent.
- Teachers of young children say that where parents have been involved in school reading projects, understand what their children are doing and how they are learning, they are less anxious and stop asking 'why can't he read yet?'*
- Parents are involved with a child's reading right from the start can co-operate well with the school.
- When parents see the satisfaction and delight children get from being offered a wide range of books, *pleasure rather than pressure* becomes the natural order.
- If you feel out of touch with your child's education, worries, anxiety and tension may follow. Becoming bound up with books at an early stage in the child's life and maintaining this interest will help you keep in touch with what is happening. If you share books, talk about books your child may be reading independently, search for and discuss information books, you will have clues about the child's progress and interest throughout school life.
- If reading is seen as a shared experience, *not an exercise or*

*E. Waterland, *Read with Me*, Thimble Press, 1985.

homework, parents are drawn closer to their children. A mutual language with common references is built up. In-jokes between you will develop. They may start with Paddington as you reach for the marmalade, and go on as the child matures past white rabbits muttering 'I'm late', and Oliver Twist asking for more to Hamlet or Macbeth. When you hear 'To tidy my room or not to . . .' be ready to reply with 'The time has come . . .'

- Parents who have varying levels of education themselves have been shown to be not only keen but *able* to give their children significant help with their reading. So do not feel that your own level of education matters. What is important is your interest. (Research studies are listed in Chapter 7.)

- Sharing books and *praising* your child will not clash with other methods of learning that may be used with the same child at the same time.

- Repeated research findings show that parents helping at home really does benefit children's reading (see Chapter 7). The young child is enthusiastic and thirsting for knowledge. Children are eager and receptive. This motivation is the single most precious commodity parents can foster and protect to help in a child's learning.

- Successful parents won't appear to be carrying out a strategy or policy, but will invite children to become co-readers – partners in the reading adventure.

COULD WE DO HARM?

Might you be going about teaching in the wrong way? Well, yes. We are far from perfect and parents do make mistakes. There are some methods we can adopt which are more successful than others. There are certainly situations we can try to avoid. Teachers frequently make certain points about parents. It's best to be aware of these, trying not to step into all the potholes along the road.

Parents are so often made to feel anxious and guilty by professionals and experts, I hope I can reassure you that the most vital element is going about something in a loving way, avoiding tension for you and your child.

Parents do have a special role and contribution, but this will certainly be of greater benefit if they avoid becoming ambitious and competitive taskmasters. Some criticism of parents is justified. A look through these comments made by teachers might help you be alert to the common complaints. I asked reception class teachers what they would like to tell parents if they could . . .

Common complaints about parents

- Parents tend to telescope their memories of how they learned to read, and often think it took them far less time than it actually did.
- Parents may have been taught that it is essential to read something 'word perfect' before going on to the next page, book or level of a reading programme. This stress on accuracy of each word rather than on the meaning of the story is less popular these days.
- You may be led into comparing one child's performance with another, either within the family or in the class.
- Anxious parents can bring tension to the whole area of reading and writing.
- Parents who are not familiar with the method of teaching being

used for their child, may seem impatient. They expect to see landmarks of progress according to their own inner idea of how this should be. So, they miss signs of progress which are less obvious.

- You may forget that children do not learn to read in a series of pre-ordained steps. Their learning ranges forward and back as diverse skills are added and others reinforced.

- You may be teaching your child to read using a method popular when you were a child. Thinking has changed. It is important to liaise with the school and take guidance from a reception teacher. However, enjoying books together, reading aloud to and with your child as I suggest here, will in no way interfere with any method.

- By being overly critical of your children's mistakes, miscues or substitutions, you may hurt their self-esteem.

- You may lack confidence and fail to realize the importance of your own contribution.

- By acts of omission, you could be signalling that you don't value reading very highly. A valued library visit may be postponed for some trivial reason, for example. If a child is reading at home are there constant interruptions? Deep down attitudes to books and reading are always picked up by children.

- Handle teachers' sensibilities with care! Some teachers appear to feel threatened or become defensive when parents are dissatisfied with a child's progress, particularly in reading.

AS EASY AS RIDING A BIKE

If you have taught a child to ride a bicycle, you will know how often you made opportunities for him to try. You supported him, running alongside the bike until he could balance alone for a few seconds. It was pretty essential that, to ride alone, he had to be on a gentle slope, facing downhill, with no major obstacles in his path. He had

to feel confident that you would not let him fall, that you were there to rely on.

By seeing others ride, he got the idea. By being supported and lovingly helped he gradually mastered it. You provided the bike of course, but also took him to a suitable place, faced the bike the correct way, helped him onto it and provided the support he needed. When he managed it you probably shouted, clapped and roared as you ran down the hill to the crumpled giggling heap at the bottom. Then the exercise had to be repeated until a panting and exhausted mum or dad could barely bring the bike back up the hill one more time.

Reading is rather like this. It finally leads to the same exhilaration as the child takes off and embarks on an adventure with literature.

Bruno Bettelheim talks of moving experiences with words leading to a 'gate of understanding' swinging open all by itself. As a result of what one reads and what feelings it evokes, it seems as if this gate opens spontaneously. Through this enchantment we can lure them to the gate.

If reading seems to offer something meaningful to them, some guide to understanding the world and the problems within it, children will go through that gate of their own accord. They will invest the effort and concentration needed (and reading is a complex skill), if they see it as leading to a worthwhile result.

If they are shown no valid reason to try and learn this skill, it is hard to believe they will make a commitment to it. If reading seems to be only about drills, flash cards and reading schemes with a limited vocabulary, it is insulting to the child's intelligence to expect that he will devote the necessary energy to it.

So, in a nutshell, it is for us as parents to motivate the child to want to read. We need to maintain a range of reading materials offering enticing books at all ages, not suddenly falling away when the child is 8 or 18 . . . We should support the child's efforts in an encouraging atmosphere with no hint that the child might 'fail'.

As when learning to ride the bike, the child has to have 'hands-on' experience of reading, trying it out and being helped when necessary – supported when he loses his balance but praised when he manages it.

2
· · · · ·

The First Five Years

FROM BABYHOOD TO SCHOOL

This is the time when the home environment has the strongest influence. Parent power is undiluted by peer group pressure, television, advertising and other competitive influences that come later.

At playgroup or nursery school books and stories form an important part of the day, but parents still have the greatest input during these years. This extraordinary power will be short-lived, so use it while you have it! Make sure that other carers who are constant in the child's life now - childminders or grannies - are aware of your ideas and aims. Make sure too that there is no pressure on the part of someone else, but that books form an integrated part of your child's experience.

By reading aloud and talking together, by sharing pictures and answering questions, you are trying to lure your child to enter the magical world of books. Your child will be developing her ability to talk and reason, to make patterns of language and thought. She will begin to know what a book is and learn the language needed - 'page', 'picture', 'word'.

LET'S EXPLORE

Watching a curious baby exploring her surroundings I am struck by how driven the child is. A desire to find out, touch, taste, pull, push and test, feeds information back to her in a constant stream.

Babies and toddlers learn at a phenomenal rate. We don't teach them as such, they learn of their own accord. We provide the secure safe environment they need and make it possible for them to learn about the world.

In between those chaotic moments when you are saving your explorer from accidents, stop to consider how many new facts this baby is taking in. It is an active process, she does not only learn from little morsels of knowledge we feed her, but from watching others and from actively doing or experimenting for herself.

Some of the happiest moments for parents come from rediscovering this exciting world as the child sees it, as if for the first time.

A mother of a 3-year-old complained: 'He's wilful, obstinate and naughty. He purposely takes too long to get ready when I want to go out and then stops along the way so many times that we never seem to arrive.' How we see this child depends on the standpoint from which we look at him. An obstinate child may drive his mother crazy but we all idolize resistance heroes from wartime.

Looked at another way, the child's determination to stop, examine and try everything is evidence of wanting to learn. An enquiring mind is a valuable asset. This drive to find out is so powerful in some babies that if we thwart the child's will regularly, we will have confrontation! To get co-operation we need to co-operate in the child's exploring.

It is easier to recognize this drive and to go with the current. If we:

- Encourage 'finding out'
- Take delight in her discoveries
- Name objects and talk about what we see and experience, we are legitimizing her full-time occupation.

Language is a vital tool for thinking. To reason, to consider and to know, your child needs words. Some people are self-conscious at first, babbling away to a person who rarely replies, but it soon becomes a two-way dialogue.

As we gradually adjust to her pace, we are humbled into not nagging when we realize what she is doing as she opens and closes the velcro strap on her shoe for the fifth time!

Pace and timing are all important to parents of toddlers. This new person needs time to experiment, to distinguish one thing from another, to learn about the shape and size of things and what you can do with them. She needs to listen to sounds, to touch, feel, taste and think. As size and shape are identified your child will embark on an intensive study of puzzles, pot and pan lids and Babushka dolls fitting one inside the other, plus all manner of 'posting' games.

HOW CAN WE HELP WITH HER FUTURE READING AT THIS STAGE?

- If we understand and enjoy her behaviour we will be encouraging and supporting the child as she grows and learns.
- This will help to build in her a *positive attitude to learning.*

- If she is happy and confident she can grow and develop.
- Language is necessary for thinking. By helping her build up her use of words, we will give her the tools she needs to communicate and consider.
- We can help her to explore different shapes and become familiar with them.

WHAT IS A BOOK?

Your baby's earliest book experiences will be in the warmth of your arms. Sitting on your lap she will explore the look and smell of books, the feel of books and even their taste! She will learn to turn a page to see something new on the other side, and she will understand that books have a right way up and a beginning and an end. Above all, this child will associate books with warmth, fun, affection and attention.

LANGUAGE IS DEVELOPING THROUGH
READING AND TALKING

Gradually the child's vocabulary grows as you name the objects seen daily at home, on outings and, of course, in books or magazines. (Babies love catalogues, especially those showing other babies.) Slowly the child will gather words together in little groups and patterns. She will form demands and those classic early sentences. As you look into pictures in picture books and talk about them, and then enjoy picture story books, language will be your tool for sharing. By reading to a small child we help to make the printed symbols of language take on meaning for her and give some idea of the purpose and pleasure of reading.

Two of the vital activities at this stage are learning to *talk* and to *distinguish*.

Simple concepts are a revelation to a toddler. The toy goes 'up' and then 'down'. Food is 'all gone' when the plate is clean. The dog is 'big' and the mouse is 'small'. As you talk together and the child grows, you will refine these words. Big and small are not always as accurate as we need to be, so fat/thin, heavy/light, wide/narrow will help as you examine things together.

Your child will want to be more precise and you will be delighted when she uses the words correctly. Talk about what you are doing, explain whenever you can.

Many games involving sorting, sizes, looking at shapes and talking about what you see will enrich your child's growing vocabulary and help to sharpen her ability to distinguish and compare what she sees.

GAMES

Touching and Talking

Can you find surfaces that have an interesting texture? Stroke a finger over a shiny smooth surface and then a rough one. Stainless steel followed by sandpaper will help your child to know rough and smooth.

Scraps of velvet and satin, fluffy fabric and fine silky scraps will be fun to compare. Talking about the sensation helps to make the words come alive.

A drop of oil on a finger leads to talk about how it feels – oily, slippery, slithery, the finger glides and slides over the others.

Shapes Everywhere

There are shapes everywhere we look. Most babies are given a 'posting' toy into which they post plastic shapes which they must match to the slots. Give a name to circles, squares and triangles. When they are posted, talk about them by name, 'There goes the diamond, into the box!' In other places around your home you can spot these shapes together. The kitchen is packed with good ones. Hold up a pot lid or a saucer and ask a two-and-a-half-year-old if it is a circle or a square. How about a square wooden board?

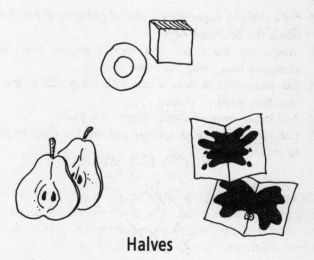

Halves

Symmetry is all around us in nature. Cut an apple or pear in half and examine them. Are they exactly the same shape on each side?

Make an ink or paint blob on a sheet of paper and fold the paper in half to make its identical copy on the folded side.

Can you tell what this is?
Remembering a shape you cannot see

Ask your child to close her eyes. Place some everyday objects in her hand one at a time and let her feel them. Can she tell you what they are?

Try this with a comb, a spoon and a toothbrush.

Make a shape game

You will need:
gummed paper shapes*, sheet of paper, pencil.

1 On a sheet of paper stick a row of gummed paper shapes down the left-hand edge.
2 Jumble up the order and stick a second row down alongside this, using the same shapes.
3 Ask your child to draw a line with the pencil to join up matching pairs of shapes.
4 Add other rows of shapes across the page.
5 Call out the name of a shape and ask the child to point to it.

Hunt for shapes

Look for cylinders, cubes, cones and spheres around the house.

---

* You can of course draw the shapes if gummed paper shapes are not available.

Spot the difference

By noticing differences in objects, the child is helped to distinguish one letter shape from another at a later stage. Some people think that if a child can tell the difference between a knife and fork she can tell the difference between letters too!

You will need:
any two pictures that are similar but not identical.

1 Use two photographs, taken one after the other, two drawings or two adverts for the same thing.
2 Your child needs time to study both pictures before pointing out all the differences she can spot.
   Keep them simple and clear.

Try a series of shapes.

b b d b

Spot the odd one

Later, once your child has got used to the game, you can use words.

was	rat
saw	rat
was	tar
was	rat

Finger paint

½ mug instant coldwater starch
½ mug soap flakes (used for hand-washing delicate articles)
⅝ mug water
powder paint

Beat these ingredients together until the mixture resembles mashed potato. Add powder paint colour. Wet your chosen surface with a wet sponge. Spread the finger paint onto shiny paper or a plastic worktop. Plastic or metal trays contain the mess slightly better. Use a spatula for spreading. Press the child's hands evenly onto the paint, then onto clean paper to print.

The same shape but facing the other way

Our hands are the same shape but face opposite ways. To experiment with this you will need:

a sheet of paper

pair of scissors

a pencil

1 Lay the child's hand onto the folded sheet of paper.
2 Draw the outline of the hand and cut out.
3 Now there are two paper hands, they can be laid one on top of the other and then arranged naturally, with thumbs inwards.

Do they look different? Can your child recognize that they are identical? Try this with fingerpaint.

Jigsaw puzzles

Puzzles will have been part of your child's life since around the end of the second year.

Sorting sizes

You will need:

two cards labelled 'big' and 'small'

big

small

pairs of objects that are large and small (think of a large dessertspoon and a teaspoon, dressmaking scissors and a pair of nail scissors. Large and small buttons, leaves, pebbles, toothbrushes, crayons, etc).

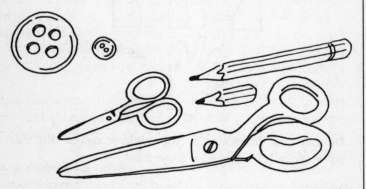

Ask your child to sort these into two piles and put the appropriate card on each pile. Alternatively, make the cards big enough to rest the objects on them.

TELL TALL STORIES

When you read aloud to small children they soon learn how a story 'works'. They will love story-making with you.

- Make up stories about the people on the bus or in the queue at the post office. Where are they going? Or what are they posting? Where will it go? Who will receive it?
- Look at the fruit stall and make up stories about the journey each fruit made from the farm to this particular stall. How did it travel? Who picked it? Were there any little insects on it?
- Using old greeting cards or postcards, let your imagination flow freely and tell stories to each other about these pictures. Write captions below them when you have decided the story. Your child will enjoy repeating this with you and alone.
- Passing a statue in the street? Who is this person? What does he or she think of the scene? (One toddler was deeply concerned about drapery apparently falling off and leaving our statue cold and shivering. Another informed me solemnly that 'of course the statue knew that London taxis were made of patent leather'.)
- Paste pictures into a scrapbook and let your child tell a story about them. Write her words beneath the pictures.
- Jumble pictures that tell a story your child knows well. Can she sort them into the right order?
- Favourite stories can be made into books. Write down the child's words and illustrate with either drawings, cut-outs from cards and magazines or in the case of a local feature take a photo such as a pond, statue or zoo.

  This book can be bound with ribbon or wool which gives added colour and, unlike staples, will not have sharp points that can work loose. Keep this special book with other books within your child's reach. It will be gazed at, handled and loved.
- Special toys might become the heroes of an ongoing serial, one episode every day. If the story is a success, it will have been repeated so often you can write it down together. For two years

we had an ongoing serial about a giraffe and his friend the giant. They went everywhere together sightseeing around London and easily looking over the heads of the crowds at any event. They could only travel in the open-topped buses and the giraffe caught a cold and sore throat this way. He ended up in St Bartholomew's hospital (it has a very high domed roof in casualty). Doctors had problems looking down his throat and getting him to say 'aah!' But, and this is the vital bit for a 3- or 4-year-old, the giraffe had a friend, a little girl who took him home and placed him in the stairwell. She poured hot drinks into him from the top floor landing and knitted him a wool scarf so that he would not catch cold on the bus again.

The child/friend in the story is always more resourceful than the adults. She always understands the toy hero better than anyone else, and the various episodes can be used to cover events in the child's life, such as going into hospital or a journey. It is easy once you start! We knitted the huge toy giraffe a warm scarf, and drew pictures of the various adventures. But mostly we used words.

RHYME AND REPETITION

Memorizing plays an important part in early reading. Choose to read stories aloud with repeated choruses, or those with cumulative texts which repeat all that has gone before. Nursery rhymes which have stood the test of time, been honed and polished by generations of children, will delight a new set of listeners. Their catchy rhymes will easily be remembered, sung or chanted. When read again and again they will gradually emerge from the blur of print into recognizable words for many readers.

Tickling rhymes, clapping and skipping rhymes are a child's heritage. When you share them, the music of patterns of words becomes etched in the memory. Cadence, intonation and rhythm enter the child's world.

Nonsense verse, far from muddling a young speaker seems to bring out a passion for precision. When a 3-year-old knows *The Owl and the Pussycat* well, try changing a few lines around. This becomes a teasing game.

And hand in foot (hand)
On the edge of the moon (sand)
They danced by the light of the sand (moon)

Two-and-a-half-year-olds fiercely love to correct this type of error on your part. Even words that sound the same, such as money and honey transposed will be spotted at once and the child will feel infinitely superior. It is sending a message to the child: look how good you are at your game of words. Daddy is rather silly. The child can believe in her own ability.

Try other nonsense verse such as Spike Milligan's *Milliganimals*.

A RICH AND VARIED READING DIET

ABCs should be within reach, some gorgeous for gazing at, others for reading aloud and some for puzzling over. Some combine nonsense verse with letters and illustration, sticking in the mind irreversibly. There are several worth owning and a wider selection may be borrowed from a library. It is not necessary to teach the alphabet order as a special drill now, let the child become familiar with the shapes of the letters and their sounds.

A pre-schooler should be thriving on a rich and wide diet of books. There will be picture books with no text. With some of these the story is very evident, in others there is room for personal interpretations. Early picture books with simple texts should include those with humour and meaningful stories. Mother Goose collections of nursery rhymes, fairy tales and verse all combine to give a newcomer to reading a glimpse of what reading books has to offer. Noise books as well as flap, cut page, pop-ups and other novelty books are skilfully made.

There is no better motivation for reading than enjoying books with someone whose enthusiasm is infectious. As the children's book market is so exciting, adults should indulge their own taste when choosing for toddlers. Look out for books you will enjoy. It will not be long before you are encouraging your child to make her own choices, holding back your opinion, so choose what you like in the first few years. In the section with useful lists and information (p.146) you will find some guides to choosing books at this age.

Be prepared for books to be handled, used, loved and occasionally damaged. If necessary mend it lovingly but don't make books 'untouchable' by toddler fingers. Keep precious books higher up, but have a good selection at toddler height. Display books where a toddler can see them and be tempted.

THE READING HABIT

Reading together is as essential now as ever, and you will need to sit with your child on your lap in such a way that she can see the words and pictures easily while watching your finger move along the page as you read or sing at a normal speaking pace.

Take a book with you in the bulging bag that all mothers of toddlers carry. Use it at odd waiting times, stave off boredom and irritability with it, surprise and delight with it, and do not mind if it becomes worn and dog-eared. Reading stories is not for bedtime only, any moment when a cuddle is called for can be a shared read. Your toddler will have clear favourites and will soon have a special book. Read it as often as she asks.

LEARNING THE ALPHABET

The letters have names, shapes and sounds. The names of the letters are not always their sounds. A is for ape but what about apple? Children can begin to play with letters and to become familiar with their shapes. It is not necessary to drill the alphabet order now, unless your child thinks it is fun. Linking the shape of the letter to its sound leads to games in which you look for things that begin with a letter always using the sound. Enjoy ABC books, write down the child's name. Let her play with writing materials unhindered. Squiggles, doodles, dots and even punctures are OK!

If your child is not interested in this ABC play, leave it alone for a while. Carry on reading together. No one learned to read by knowing the alphabet alone. *Books* make readers.

FASCINATION WITH PRINT

Those squiggles on the page are now familiar and the child will recognize letters in adverts on the back of the bus, a road sign or a cereal pack. Painted words in the road such as 'Stop' will have a child transfixed at the kerb. Words are often guessed at because the first letter is recognized. Excited shouting from the back seat will tax your driving skills as your child recognizes a letter on a shopfront or hoarding. Then there are ice-cream signs and hamburger store logos . . .

GAMES

Learning letters

Letter friezes allow children to gaze at the letter shapes from time to time, almost unconsciously noticing their distinctive shapes. Put up a frieze in the kitchen or in a child's room.

Spot letters

Spot letters everywhere in print around your home, in the street, on vehicles, signs, tickets and newspapers. Some letters are found in different styles - try to spot these as a game. Circle them when you see them in a newspaper, catalogue or magazine.

Play another spotting game, seeing who can spot the most instances of the letter you call out.

Making letters

Create letters out of every material you have to hand. Encourage children to 'write' the shape by passing fingers over it. (See diagram showing which direction to use on page 94.)

1 Cut from sandpaper, glossy magazine covers, fluffy fabric, felt offcuts.
2 Mould from Plasticine or playdough, Fimo or other modelling clay.
3 Draw with fingers on steamy mirrors or windows.
4 Draw with a stick in wet sand on a beach or in a sandpit.
5 Use a piece of string to make letters.

Games

- Play snap with alphabet cards.
- Play bingo with alphabet cards.

- Play *Fetch Me* . . . Ask a child to fetch you a number of things which begin with the letter . . . (Use the sound rather than the name of the letter at first: if you are expecting an apple don't say A as in ape, but say it as in hat.)

Always keep these suggestions as games for fun - never let them become drills, or 'reading exercises'. Don't mention that they will help with reading or are for reading. Reading must remain a special treat with a book.

3
· · · · ·

Towards Reading

WHEN IS YOUR CHILD READY?

'Reading readiness' is a term parents remember from their schooldays. When is a child ready and what does ready imply? Parents may be afraid to encourage a child to read too soon. If he is not yet ready, they wonder, how can we help him become ready?

There used to be elaborate tests to determine reading readiness. Fixed ages were suggested as though children ripened like fruit to a specific age of readiness. But we know that reading is not learned in rigid steps at a set moment with a programme of stages towards success. We learn to read gradually and by many different methods. We don't all learn at the same pace.

The toddler looking at a picture book and turning the page to see the next picture has, in a sense, begun already because he has an idea of the purpose of reading. Small children who badger their parents for 'one more bedtime story, please!' are well on the way to becoming avid readers. They have learned the excitement of stories unfolding within a book. They know too that a favourite story remains inside the book to return to time and again. So, children as young as the toddler are ready for you to share books with them, though they may not be ready to read independently.

When parents and teachers talk about reading readiness, they often mean that a child is ready to begin to learn to read *aloud* independently. A child may, in fact, be silently recognizing names of favourite characters on the page and key words as you read to him. He has begun to read. To be ready in the school sense though, he needs to be able to understand the instructions his teacher gives him. He will need to know where the beginning of the page is, and the difference between a word and a letter. So this question of readiness involves not only reading print, but a wide range of 'know-how' about language.

WHAT DOES YOUR CHILD KNOW ABOUT THE PROCESS OF READING?

Your child may be making meaning from print well before he goes to school, but the method the teacher uses to teach reading may be new to him. If he has been recognizing words and the teacher places more emphasis on sounds, he may not *seem* 'ready to read' because he is trying so hard to follow her instructions that he cannot concentrate on the shape of the words as he did before.

One child may have a strong eye for shapes, but not a developed ear. He may not recognize sounds that are alike as easily as a second child who recognizes words with similar sounding first letters, but who is less good at recognizing shapes. One child is no more ready than another, as both have begun to read. They need to build upon their strengths and receive help with other facets of their learning.

There are children who seek the meaning hidden in print by puzzling out what words and sentences might be from the sense of it. Certain early readers have memorized much-loved stories and they begin simply to 'see' the words that are familiar on the page. There are many ways of coming towards reading.

Each child has begun to read without any external measurement of readiness. Each child needs to make the most of his abilities while broadening reading skills. Fortunately there is *no rigid, single way* to teach or learn reading. The good, fluent readers studied by researchers seem, in fact, to have taught themselves to read regardless of the methods adopted in their classroom.

Reading is achieved by a combination of our hereditary ability, our growth, experience and our learning. When these fuse into an awareness of what is involved in reading, and a desire to do this for oneself, the child is a beginner.

A BEGINNER

The word 'beginner' is important. No beginners at any skill can perform perfectly, nor are they expected to. Reading dawns on children; print gradually appears meaningful. What we can do to help them is be supportive and provide learning opportunities. We need to offer a wide range of tempting reading material and a chance to try to be a reader in safety. We should bring no tension to this. There should be no invisible measuring which poses a risk of failing; no comparing with another child. Most of us expect our children to learn to talk and they do. We did not measure their readiness to speak, we were overjoyed at their attempts. It should be the same for reading.

What we can do is always *treat a child as a reader* at all stages.

- A beginner is a reader in every sense and, as such, deserves the respect we accord a reader.
- He can become ready to read at an early age or reach this point a little later than his friends.
- There is no set number of years and months which will automatically produce readiness in a child.

THE WELL-READ INFANT

Real reading encourages thought and stretches the imagination. Readers encounter the mind of the author and meet new ideas and experiences. A well-read infant knows about far more than he can have experienced directly. *Books have made him ready for reading.*

At a risk of stating the obvious, a child is ready to read *because he wants to.* He has discovered that it is exciting and entertaining to hear new stories. It is comforting and reassuring to return to familiar favourites. He knows stories remain in the text and pictures for him to unlock. He is beginning to realize that he can extract meaning from print in books and all around him.

He is starting to match seeing with saying. Print all around him, at home, in books, in the street, on vans, on cereal packets and in shops begins to hold his attention. He asks 'What does it say?' because he knows there is meaning locked in print. Children unlock the meaning of store logos, signs and adverts on television. They look at the label on their dungarees and collect stickers. They tell makes of car apart. Occasionally he will say 'that says Stop!' or 'that says Way In' with the excitement of discovery. You have not yet decided he is ready to learn to read – *he has decided and has begun.* Parents are called upon to be enthusiastic and admiring as he surges on, guessing, stumbling and getting it right.

LET THE CHILD LEAD THE WAY

It is most important that he seizes and keeps this initiative. Some children, being force-fed drill and exercises, perceive reading as something done to them by adults and wait passively for reading to happen to them. The best readers are those who grasp reading for themselves. If you boost a child's confidence from these first efforts it will carry him over obstacles and he will know that he can tackle print despite occasional setbacks.

RANGING BACK AND FORTH

The beginner wants a variety of reading experiences. He may be retelling a story he has memorized from a loved, familiar book. He retells the story and recognizes landmarks and some words on the page, turning over at the right point. We listen to his retelling, and read it in turn when asked, no matter how many times, for this is reinforcing his new knowledge and confirming it for him. Don't be too impatient to change from a book your child wants again and again. It may be from this very book that he will reach a breakthrough in reading. He is not bored by it even if you are!

His choice will range backward and forward and occasionally he will choose picture books with no text at all. He will love to read his own words which he has dictated to you.

SHARING THE BOOK

Sit together with the child comfortably on your lap or next to you. Let the beginner follow your reading as you point to the words, reading at a natural steady pace and with expression. When you come to a line he knows well, pause and let him say or read it. Little by little he will read more and you will read less.

KEEP CALM!

An over-enthusiastic parent may, at the first signs of reading, be a little pushy through eagerness to help. Take it easy!

- Let the child choose when to stop.
- Never insist that he read to you, even if he can. If he wants you to read to him tonight, simply do so.
- If, however, he stops reading himself for a while, try reading an old favourite with a chorus of repetition that he knows by heart.

Begin to read and, when you reach the chorus, stop and turn to him to supply the missing words. A few of these successful shared reads may bring back his nerve to try again for himself.

- He may want to read aloud with you in unison.
- Keep to stories he knows well so that his first efforts will succeed.
- Don't keep stopping him and correcting.

Let him read for sense. If what he reads makes sense, even if it is a substitution, it means he has read and understood. Only help if he is stuck for a word, then simply say the word quietly so that he can continue.

Praise often. When listening to a new reader it is easy to speak only when there is something to be corrected and to remain silent while the child reads. *This new reader needs constant praise and encouragement.*

USE RHYME AND RHYTHM

The child will link saying or singing with seeing through nursery rhymes and chants. Choose the best Mother Goose you can find, and return to it, now that your child knows many of the tales by heart from toddler days. He will now be finding the right page for you and recognizing names like Jack or Simon or Baa Baa Black Sheep. Let your child inherit the oral tradition of English that has been loved by so many generations of children. The chants and rhythms will work their way into his memory. Early tickles and finger games will be known by heart. Amazingly, even a 4-year-old has a past you can refer to.

Share the reading of repetitive and cumulative stories. These are easy to memorize and predict. Stop and fade out when you come to the well-worn lines. This is your child's turn. Soon the new reader will take over more than these phrases. Pointing with the finger helps keep the eye on the right place in the line of print.

Point while you read so that your child can follow.

As he begins to read more words and phrases, carry on in the same way, reading together, always fading out or stopping when the child wants to read alone. Pick up and continue when he needs you to. In this way a text is not too hard for the child because you are there to move the story forward and he reads what he can with no risk of failure.

He may like reading in unison, your voices joining together. Soon he will recognize words he knows when he sees them in a new context. A 3- or 4-year-old loves repetition, is not bored by it as a 5-year-old might be. This makes it easy for the child to know a book by heart. It is the much loved and oft repeated books that form the breakthrough to reading which seems such a miracle.

BREAKTHROUGH

When this moment is reached there can be little doubt. Children seem to fall in love with print. Not only storybooks, but newspaper headlines, advertisements, labels, packets, messages and notices. The world suddenly seems filled with messages in written form.

The reward for the effort of reading should be a good story. Give the child a book written in a lively style and with witty or beautiful illustrations. Make sure he does not get bogged down in repetitive, structured 'readers'. Drills and readers designed to teach reading are often tedious for the child to read, and for the adult to listen to, for by now, you will frequently be listening attentively while your child reads with you. Glance through the chapter, *Choosing is everything*, page 121. Remain ready to quietly say a word when he gets stuck. Make no great fuss, but try to keep the sense of the story going. Do not stop him to correct a wrong word if it has the correct meaning.

If the child reads pony for horse, you know he has, in fact, read the word horse and understood it. If he says house for horse then the sense is lost. It is often helpful to wait until the child finishes the sentence, when he may realize for himself that it did not make sense and correct himself. If not, gently ask about the meaning of the sentence. *Reading for meaning is vital* if children are not to stop hearing the sense of the story as they recite words, simply doing a decoding exercise. Talk about the story, try to predict what might happen next and remind your child what happens if you have read this before.

INSULTING MATERIAL

There may be a difference between the child's spoken vocabulary and the words he can read. This can lead to the child being given books to read which insult his intelligence. This seems to be a danger at 6, or 7, when the child is very alert and aware of the world through television, school and home life. Once you *can* read, *what* you read is crucial. Before you can read, what you're offered must *make reading seem worthwhile.*

One bright 7-year-old was reading a classic novel at home, considered by most adults to be too high-brow, while plodding through a structured reading scheme at school. But the teacher insisted he progress through all the levels of the scheme despite being already beyond it. He was lucky to have parents who offered him books he could really enjoy. If his only experience of reading had been the readers, he might well have been bored by reading.

MY CHILD IS 5½ AND HAS NOT YET REACHED THE BREAKTHROUGH STAGE

If your child has not yet reached this stage and is 5 or 6, simply carry on reading together in a loving, happy way. Check that the books you share are interesting, exciting, humorous and inviting. As the child reaches 5, tastes may change and stories filled with action are often more popular. Read through the chapter *Choosing is everything* on page 121 and try to remain supportive and calm without comparing your child to any other.

- If your child has started school, do you know what the school's policy is on reading?
- You might find that your child is learning fast in some other area such as numbers, and is not thinking much about reading.
- Some children put all their energy into coping socially at school in the first term or two. Is he relaxed and happy at school?
- Have a chat with the child's teacher, try to form a partnership with her and come to a better understanding of what she is trying to do in the area of reading and writing (see page 79). Your child will benefit if there is a united approach with school and home both supporting his attempts.
- If you are at all worried about your child's hearing or vision, have them checked. They are checked at school, but if you are at all concerned that something is amiss, don't hesitate to seek medical advice.
- Some children suffer temporary hearing loss after a heavy head cold.
- Any major upheavals in life will affect a young child in many ways. An illness or emotional crisis in the family can set him back.
- Children reach this breakthrough stage over a wide age range.

GAMES

Make your own books

- Many books can be made at home. Choose an excellent picture book without text, and with your child, develop a story around the pictures. Write the child's words out clearly.

- You might like to record them on tape too.
- A picture book with a simple text is easily 'translated'. Write out the text clearly in the translated form.
- Write down an account of a day at home, an outing or a festival and add a few pictures. Snapshots of the family or drawings can be put together to make a personal and attractive little book. Bind the book with brightly coloured wool or ribbon rather than use staples. Many print shops offer a comb binding cheaply.
- Look at the ideas in Let's use writing and Share the importance of writing on page 69, and Special letters on page 73.

BILINGUAL PARENTS

You will have the double riches of two cultures' fables and folklore, games and rhymes to introduce. Follow the suggestions described in this chapter in the language you have chosen to speak to the child since birth. If this language is not that of public print, in this case English, you will have to counter pressure from television and advertisements, from signs such as 'entrance' and 'way out'. It helps to have a wide range of reading materials available now. Some can be made at home.

Many books are now available in dual language editions. Look carefully through bookshop shelves in English on the fables and cultures of other lands which you can translate for your child. Check with your local library for anything they may have or be able to order in your language. Check through the lists on page 146 for magazines or organizations that could help you.

Consider carefully how your child will cope with school. Which language will be used? Before your child receives any formal teaching of reading you will need to have some discussions with his teacher or playgroup leader. You will want to be assured that your own language is accepted and treated with respect by the teacher even if the child is to be taught in English.

It is vital for parents whose home language is not English to establish a dialogue with the school or nursery.

WHAT CAN I DO IN ONLY A FEW MINUTES AFTER WORK?

You can teach children the ABC, the shape, name and sound of letters, but in itself, this can never make them real readers. Only the joy of sharing books will do this. So, if the nagging question at the back of your mind is, 'I only have a few minutes with him after work, what should I concentrate on? Flashcards? Alphabet? Nursery rhymes? Writing? Stories?', the answer can only be - share a book together, one you can enjoy too. Finish a story at a sitting. Try to make this time special for you both. Talk about the story, share the emotion, the humour and the beauty of the pictures. Above all share the pleasure of each other's company and your delight in the story.

If something in a book is relevant to your lives, this is a chance to talk about it. Children can be reassured by stories. Finding out that characters are scared of the dark, for instance, or afraid of becoming lost, may help the child to talk about his own feelings. Don't hurry this precious time.

If it is impossible for you to do this, can you ask another patient adult who spends a fair amount of time with your child? An older child or a grandparent may volunteer his attention for just the length of time that pleases them both. They will both derive satisfaction from a good read.

If you do manage to read with your child frequently, but want something to fall back on in an emergency, record some of the favourite stories onto tape. This is no substitute for your own warmth and presence, but you could use it when necessary. The child may enjoy looking through the book and listening to your voice telling the familiar tale.

If time is short do try to make reading together a priority. Childhood is all about memories. Make some together with quality time even if quantity is not possible.

WHAT TO DO AS READING DAWNS ON YOUR CHILD

As you become aware of your child's enthusiasm for reading words and phrases independently, it is not necessary to 'teach' him to read.

- Continue to share books, making certain that when you read together your child is comfortable and can see the print and the pictures.
- Point to the words as you read them at normal speed.
- Look 'into' the pictures together. In some books the pictures give clues to the text, in others they offer a joke to the reader. In Janet and Allan Ahlberg's *The Great Marathon Football Match* (HarperCollins, 1992), the text reads:
'All the boys worked very hard.
They got their mothers to sort out old clothes and make some cakes for the cake stall.'

The three comic-style pictures on the page show the boys not working hard at all, while their mothers slave under piles of jumble. And in a hot kitchen, as one mother wipes her fevered brow her son (reading the paper, legs crossed on a chair) is helping himself to a biscuit.

The sense of superiority a child feels when he is 'in the know' boosts his confidence. He sees himself as a reader, able to discern meaning in the book. Pat Hutchin's *Rosie's Walk* (Penguin, 1970) also offers the reader a joke while the text goes steadily on, seemingly unaware.

- Leave unhurried time for discussion before you turn over a page. Talk about any special words. A word may be unknown, it may sound just like what it says, it may be a word in which a child takes delight. Children enjoy words and may want to talk about other words that mean the same thing.

- 'Can you guess what will happen next?' is a question that focuses on the story, the main purpose of reading. Predicting what might come next helps the reading.
- Once you have read the story to your child, he might tell it to you in his turn. This may be a simple retelling of the sequence in his words. He may recite it from memory, or he may memorize it *and* also use key words or landmarks on the page to know when to turn over or where he is in the text. He may read some words or phrases, as you read it again. This is certainly not 'cheating' as some parents fear. It is a valid form of early reading.
- *Praise all efforts your child makes.*
- Offer a wide range of tempting books. Return often to old favourites.

CHECKLIST

DON'T say:

You've met that word so many times before, you should know it by now.

You weren't listening! I explained it already!

You ought to be reading a harder book.

I thought we said we'd read every afternoon.

Stop that! Come and do reading now.

Don't fidget, pay attention.

You will need to be able to read when you grow up.

DO:

Praise your child often.

Value his work, drawings, writing and story-telling. Display it when possible.

Share books for enjoyment at a moment when the child is willing.

Listen to what the child is saying.

Talk to the child as you would to an intelligent and sensitive adult.

Respect the child's taste in books.
Take great care in choosing books to suit the child.
Spend as much time with the child as you can. Time spent with a child is time well spent.

NO SITTING IN JUDGEMENT

If we keep in mind that we are sharing a book, not sitting in judgement on the child's performance, we will not be waiting to stop him and correct a 'mistake'. We need to put our attention to the story, laughing if it is funny, enjoying any expression or special effects the child adds to the telling of it. If the meaning of the story is uppermost, the child will realize if he has made a mistake because the sense will be affected. Wait until he reads to the end of a sentence and notices this. Usually he will correct himself. If he doesn't, talk about the story and ask about that sentence and its meaning. If the child sticks at a difficult word simply say it quietly and keep the story moving. Make certain that your comments are not only corrective. Do you often say 'That's good!' or even 'How did you read that difficult word?'! It is all too easy to be silent while the child reads correctly and to interrupt only to point out a mistake.

BUILD A HOME LIBRARY

Visits to the library will widen your child's range of reading material, but there is no substitute for owning some books – the very best ones, of course. On my daughter's shelves stand 40-year-old copies of my childhood favourites. *Madeleine, Eloise and Babar* jostle *Black Beauty, The Snow Goose, Heidi* and *Winnie the Pooh*. They share the shelf with her brother's battered copies of *Gumdrop*, Richard Scarry titles and *How It Works* volumes. She stands these books alongside her best books, weeding out those she does not

think worthy of shelf space. Over the years some books are given away, but the best are kept, regardless of the age group for which they are intended.

Children's books are inexpensive if you keep them in use! Many can be found second-hand and in paperback. If you build up a collection gradually, say a book each month and a few for birthdays and other treats, your child will be able to return to the stories that have made a special impact time and again. These books will be significant. They have entered your child's life, drifted with him into sleep and become part of his experience. Children will enjoy the feeling of ownership, handling the book and returning to it at will to pore over the illustrations, or to let the sounds of its words 'curl into their ears and veins like soft mists . . . and the mists will cling and the children will grow into the sounds and the memory of them . . .'*

TASTES WILL RANGE BACK AND FORTH

At this time there may be a wide gap between your child's spoken vocabulary and the range of words he can read independently. But

---

*Keri Hulme, *The Bone People*, Pan Books, 1986.

books chosen for him should not be too simple. When he needs help you will read to him and with him. This way you will enlarge his use of the language, helping with words he has not met or cannot guess. You will mix the books, offering those that are easy for him to read, and some you expect to read to him.

Difficult material may catch his interest – something about football in the newspaper perhaps – but there will be other days when you will share a textless picture book or pop-up. A fluent reader may return from a library visit with a simple text that is a novelty. He does not have to be reading in graded stages, ever harder. Let a new reader find out about the pleasure of a wide choice of books.

A BOOK WITHOUT WORDS WHEN HE HAS BEGUN TO READ?

Books without words such as *The Snowman,* by Raymond Briggs (Hamish Hamilton, 1978), can mean different things to various readers. Each child brings to it his own level of understanding and word skill. He will learn story-telling conventions by retelling the story. As the child follows the exploits of the characters he must keep and connect the episodes in sequence. He must describe the action and the setting, link cause and effect, examine the evidence in the picture, notice fine details and tell this to you in an entertaining manner. He becomes a story-teller.

Some stories permit deeper levels of meaning to be brought out, linking them to universal issues that affect us all. This is typically true of Briggs as author and illustrator.

You may feel disappointed when a child who has begun to read for himself, selects a book like this. But there is no 'shirking' in the enjoyment of any aspect of a book. There is no 'cheating' either when a child is 'reading' something he has memorized. These are all valuable steps towards reading.

Handling books

- If a child makes his own book, or you write down his words, keep it among real books on the shelf. Make sure he knows his effort is as good as the bought product.
- Make up ideal stories to suit a certain child.
- Books are to be handled and enjoyed. The odd marks of wear and tear are inevitable. Respect books but don't make them untouchable.
- Keep books within the child's reach. Display them attractively.

A few comfortable cushions or a generous armchair invite you to curl up with a book. These points may seem too obvious to mention, but so often books are out of reach and the child cannot simply lie and stare at the covers until one tempts him to get it down. Many adults remember how they lay in bed gazing at their books thinking of stories and planning which one to read next.

Finding books

- Ask librarians and booksellers for advice on books. Good booksellers, especially those in children's bookshops, will have read the books.
- Local libraries are increasingly preparing lists to help parents in their choice of books.
- There are guides for sale on good books for your children (see page 147).
- Book reviews in the press and specialist publications can be useful.
- Talk to teachers, other families and older children.
- Through your library you can find out about established children's books. You can then look for these in second-hand shops and markets.

GOALS TO AIM AT

As the early stages draw towards school-days and a breakthrough in reading, it is useful to bear in mind certain goals. These are not fixed rules. It does not matter if your child cannot pass a mythical test. They are simply worth aiming at sooner or later.

- As always, the most important: motivate children to want to read. In order to want to read they need to know a little of what reading and writing is all about - what pleasure there is in it, and how useful it is in everyday life. *Not* how useful it will be to them one day. (See Early writing, page 95 and Use your child as a scribe, page 98).
- They need to know that reading is done from left to right and from the top of the page to the bottom.
- They need to know the difference between 'word' and 'letter'.
- It helps to know the alphabet but especially the shapes of the letters and their sounds.
- They need to know the language of teaching and how to follow instructions, 'start at the beginning', 'the one below', 'behind', 'in front of'.

Keep the pleasure of reading and sharing worthwhile books as your main goal. Make children into readers and then improve skills. Skills alone do not produce readers because no drill or game can get across to a child the reason for trying to decipher the words on a page. It is only by introducing a child to literature of the best kind, that we 'advertise' the purpose of reading. Games and pre-reading activities all have their place but are purposeless without real books and reading.

Don't blunt the pleasure of reading and listening to good stories by pointing out facts about letters and words in the middle of an exciting story. An over-eager adult may seize every opportunity to teach and in this way spoil relaxation and concentration.

By all means sharpen a child's skills through games. When a child discovers he can do something, he naturally wants to practise it at every opportunity. It is like skipping or riding a bicycle, once you've got it, you think of nothing else for a time.

Learning letter shapes and sounds is good fun. Play games with letters and with words, but don't let this take over from reading and don't call it 'reading games'. A game is simply that, a game played for fun and when a child feels like it.

For some children the fascination with word games comes later when they can read and have a large vocabulary. You will have years of Scrabble ahead. Take it gently with your 3- or 4-year-old.

One of the best 'games' for this age group is having a good listener while they struggle to get a long elaborate tale in sequence. It may not be easy to have the patience to hear out this child but it is very important to him. It is also tiring to answer the endless questions of a 3-year-old, but showing respect for his intelligence requires that you try to concentrate and find out a valid answer even if you do not know it now. (Some of us get re-educated through our children!) In one day you may face how records are made and why there are holes in cheese. Add to this some quick facts on electricity and mirrors and you are doing well.

You are indirectly helping his reading and all his future learning. Perhaps the answers lie in a helpful book? If you turn to one of the many illustrated *How and Why?* books for answers, your child learns to look in books for information and to satisfy his curiosity. I felt out of my depth so frequently that I had to seek help from car mechanics, stable hands and firemen to answer these searching questions, but books formed the most useful resource.

GAMES

Alphabet games

Buy a set of alphabet cards or make your own. Use stiff card and print each letter with a thick marker pen. Sticky plastic covers will extend their life. Initially, make a set of lower-case cards. Later you can make a second set with upper-case letters, and one set in which each card has both upper- and lower-case examples.

Leave alphabet books lying open where the child can see them. Have plastic letters available for him to handle and make letters from Plasticine or other modelling clay, pipe cleaners, string, sandpaper, velvet scraps and other materials which he can feel. Encourage a child to make the letter you are currently talking about for himself, using some of these materials. Let him use a wet finger on paving slabs, a finger on steamy glass, finger paint, sand in a shallow tray, crayons on textured paper or a magic slate. A keyboard of either a typewriter or a personal computer is fascinating to a child.

- Let him feel a letter while blindfolded and guess which one it is.
- Teach jingles or nonsense verse and play guessing games with these.
- Let him match up lower-case cards with upper-case ones.
- On cards with both upper- and lower-case letters, cut each card in half and have the child match them up again.
- With two sets of alphabet cards play a game of 'snap'.
- Sing the alphabet song to the tune of *Twinkle, twinkle little star*. Write it down on pages to form a special alphabet book.
- After looking through several alphabet books make up your own personal family version . . . one child offered 'D is for Danny who dribbles and drips'! The baby gurgled happily at this, for the moment!
- With two or three sets of alphabet cards, play a matching game. Offer the child three cards, two identical, the third another letter. Have him match up the two which are alike.

Talking about letters and sounds

Write down the child's name. Ask:

1 'Do you know any other person whose name starts the same way as yours?'
2 'Do you know the name of the letter at the beginning of this name?'
3 'Have you come across any other word that begins with this letter?'
4 'Can you hear that these words all start with the same sound?'
5 'Can you tell me the sound these names start with?'
6 'Can you add any more words that start this way?'

Words are written down and read over several times. Leave this sheet where the child can see it. Days later your child may recognize this letter on an advert or shop sign. He will be alerted to its shape and sound. Help him to spot the letter and when words crop up with this sound, talk about them from time to time.

It is easier to begin with sounding consonants. They vary less than vowels in the sound they represent, and there is less variation due to local dialect or home language spoken.

Using short words, listen to the initial sounds made by consonants.

Pre-readers games

Small children are strongly attracted to any idea using their names. They are happy to be drawn into a game when it is personalized in this way. Capitalize on this fascination and help a child to recognize the letters that form his name.

1 Make name labels and use them for places at the table or put them on a piece of cake or fruit saved for someone. Sort a heap of family belongings (laundry, stray objects) into piles for each person.
   Make a name tag into a bracelet or a badge.
   Write names on paper napkins.
   Write names inside Wellingtons.
2 When a child can recognize his own name, let him pick his own from a pile of names. Slowly he will come to recognize letters that form his name and appear in other names too. Spotting these becomes a new game.
3 Can you think of any friends' names that start with the same sound? The child may say George, John, Janine. This is for sound only so the use of G or J is acceptable.

4   Stick a snapshot of each family member onto a sheet of paper, clearly writing their names beneath. By looking at this often, the child will come to know the shapes of these names. He already knows the name that goes with each photo, so the initial sound in that person's name will be easy to identify.

5   Using the letters that go to make up the child's name, try to think of words that start with the sound of each letter. Write these clearly down beneath his name. This game can vary by using different categories of words.

- Play it with names of children.
- Play it with general words.
- Play it as a search game in the home (look for something beginning with each of these sounds . . . the child can walk around the house with a list of the sounds and look).
- When travelling in the car play it as a variety of 'I spy'. Look out and spy something starting with one of the sounds, then ask the child to find others.
- When on a shopping trip, pick a letter and ask a child to see how many objects he can spot starting with it.
- Write a child's name with each letter on a separate card. Have the child rearrange these in the right order.

Naming letters

Learning the names of the letters is much easier when you sing the alphabet song together. Repetition rhythm and rhyme are great aids. Write out the alphabet as the song is arranged, and make little books out of this.

'*abcdefg, hijklmnop, qrs* and *tuv, w* and *xyz* now you know your abc, you can come and play with me.' (sung to *Twinkle, twinkle little star*). The American 'zee' rhymes better than 'zed', of course.

The shopping list

Together have a discussion about your shopping list. Carefully write out a list of what you need. Make a card for each item and leave the cards at home. While in the store your child can tick the items off your list as you find them. When you get the goods home, your child can try to label the items using the cards.

In this way he sees and says the words several times in context. If the mood is one of a treasure hunt, and more than one child joins in, it can become a regular treat.

WHAT IS A WORD?

Many children confuse the meaning of word and letter at first. Explain what a word is and how you write it, leaving a space on either side of it before starting another one. Show that words consist of individual letters whose sounds together will make up this word. It is helpful to do this with two simple words at first, for instance 'very hot'.

Children hear spoken language flowing together. Phrases cling to each other and words appear to flow into each other. A surprising number of small children think 'How are you?' is one word. There are several phrases they hear every day and they pick up language so quickly incorporating the total phrase in their growing vocabulary. Years later you may discover that your child thinks of 'once upon a time' or 'happily ever after' as he hears it spoken, in one word.

Make it clear that English is read and written from left to right and from top to bottom of the page. A child coming to school without this knowledge will be severely set back when told by a teacher to start at the beginning. Some teachers, while trying to teach the alphabet, find that children do not all understand the meaning of words like 'before' and 'after' as in 'what letter comes before c?' It will be of great value to your child to know the language of teaching and to be familiar with simple instructions.

Looking at a page of print, you can talk about how the lines are arranged on the page, and explain that the end of a line does not always mean the end of a group of words called a sentence. A complete thought expressed in words is said to be a sentence. This is extremely difficult for very young readers to understand. You might like to say that at the end of the sentence, where you see the full stop dot, there is a chance to stop, breathe and think about what is coming next. One idea has been explained. Another is coming. Ask the child to give you a sentence about what he had for breakfast and print it clearly running on to a second line, then put a full stop. The next sentence might be about a different idea, how you went to school or to the shops. This helps, but do not worry if this concept takes a long while to register.

GAMES

Concepts

Play games with the concepts of above and below, over and under, in front and behind, through and around. Use counters or toys and ask your child to put blue, say, on top of green, or teddy behind Mary.

on top of

behind

through

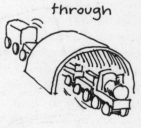

SHARE THE IMPORTANCE OF WRITING

- We can preserve and keep information by writing it down. If we write down what we did today, we can remind ourselves of it next week when we have forgotten.
- Talk disappears . . . writing remains.
  Make a record of the weather. Did it rain last Wednesday? Did it rain the week before that?
- Write a letter to gran or a friend and post it together.

- Use writing as a reminder. Write 'Katie is coming to tea on Friday', and stick it on the fridge or a bulletin board. Your child might tick off the days until Friday on a calendar or simply write the names of the days as they pass.
- Stick a leaf or feather into a scrapbook. Write underneath what it is and where you found it.

Let's use writing

- Most exciting of all, writing can be used to capture your child's own words on paper. When he tells you about something that happened to him today, you can write it out for him as his own personal story, and he can read it again and again in his own words. Children often need adults to act as scribes who write down whatever they dictate. Everyone enjoys reading about himself or hearing a story in his own words. It is a most satisfying form of reading, made easier by the fact that the words are used in the natural pattern that the child would normally use. He knows the words and what comes next. Add a few pictures drawn by the child, or snapshots of the day and it is the best book ever. Bind with coloured wool or ribbon.

... and then we went on the bus ...

- Show a child how writing is useful to us every day. Have him write down two or three names of close friends or family you contact most often (he may need to copy these from your clear printing). Write their telephone numbers next to their names. Each time you need to ring one of them, have your child help you look up the name and dial the number.
- Draw a chart showing how tall your children are. Write their names clearly. Teddies may wish to be measured too. Familiar written words, such as names of people or toys she knows, help the child place the concepts more easily in context than individually on a card.

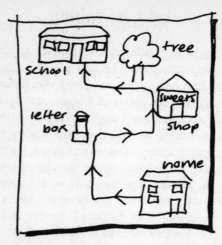

- Do you walk to school, the postbox or shops? Draw a diagram of your route and write clearly, letter box, shops, street pavement, big tree or other landmarks you see each day. You can tell each other stories about how you get ready and set off down the road, round the corner to the end of the street, up the hill and there is the letter box. Write out 'round the corner' or 'up the hill' as a group of words together. Don't forget 'put on our wellies, or mittens and hat', and use everyday words and phrases your child knows well and understands.

  Your child can tell you the story, putting the actions in the right sequence. If the actions are written out on cards (groups of words) he can try to put a well-known story in order. It is his special story. This story can be embroidered as he stands 'on tip-toe' at the letter box or lists what you bought at the shops. Finally there is 'turn around', and 'set off for home'.

Special letters

Letters are so loved by small children as they pop through the slot in the front door or into the box. They are always upset that they don't receive letters every day like adults do. When they do get a letter it is so special it is usually kept and gazed at for days.

If you do not have a special person you could ask to send your child a few letters, some very exciting ones can come from book characters. Geraldine Taylor in *Be Your Child's Natural Teacher* (Penguin, 1987) tells how she had a son hooked on Peter Pan. She wrote letters to him and a marvellous correspondence started.

We had a favourite story for a time about Ralph the Rhino who dined at the Ritz. He was a gourmet and a detective. Inadvertently I came across some Ritz stationery while on holiday and dashed off a letter saying I had met Ralph at the Ritz, etc., etc.

Could Paddington get a letter from darkest Peru? There is no end to the possibilities! Use typewriters, word processors or your own printing, but keep the text very clear. The child will puzzle out the meaning of this very special letter. You may be asked to write or help with his reply.

GAMES

Alphabet play

- Stencil or draw letters onto paper, and encourage your child to colour the spaces between the letters. This can be in patterns, dots or stripes or flat areas of colour. The letters you have drawn should stand out against the background of pattern and colour. This will give the child a good idea of the shapes and plenty of time to play around the letters with doodles and colouring.
- Cut a letter shape from stiff paper or card. Lay it on a sheet of paper. Have your child dip an old toothbrush into some prepared watercolour or powder paint. By scraping a spatula (lolly stick) against the bristles a finely spattered mist of colour will fall around the stencilled shape. When

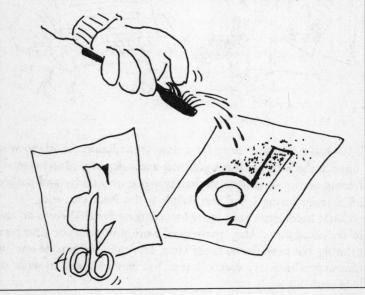

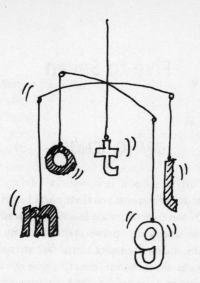

you lift it off it will stand out in the colour of the paper against the background. Always place the work in the bottom of a cardboard grocery carton, then spattering will not cover every available surface. Keep the toothbrush on the dry side. When one colour is dry, apply a second. You might try the child's name this way.

- Make a mobile from cut-out card letters attractively coloured and patterned by children. Hang each letter with a wool thread or pretty ribbon. Wind ribbon around all the sides of a wire hanger and suspend the letters from it on different lengths. Letters like G can have other letters hooked into them.

4
. . . . .

Five to Seven

OFF TO SCHOOL

So your baby is off to school! It is with a mixture of pride and apprehension that many parents see their child begin school. If you have taken care to see that the child is well prepared you will both feel happier. Little things can prove awkward. Can she undo the stiff button on her shorts for toilet visits? What type of shoes did you choose? Can she do them up herself? Does the child have any experience of being in a group? Waiting her turn for the teacher's attention, or holding her own when she is being teased – these skills are often learned at playgroup or nursery. When you visit the school with the child before term begins, show her where the pegs or lockers are, and where the toilets are in relation to the room she will be in.

If you see a book you both know displayed in this new classroom, point it out to your child. A friendly book is like a familiar face. Make certain that you both know exactly where you will wait to pick up the child at the end of the session.

KEEP CALM AND POSITIVE

Deal with these things matter-of-factly. There is no point in passing on any niggling worries to a 5-year-old. Let her believe she will manage easily, because she has discussed these matters with you beforehand. It helps if she sees you chatting easily with her new teacher. If she feels that you like the teacher, she will expect to like her herself. Going to school each morning is a ritual you will both face. It can become a very special time as you walk or travel together. Time to chat, to notice what sort of day it is, what the trees look like and what the ants are carrying across the pavement. As your child gets older she may love to play 'not stepping on the lines' or 'I spy'. This time defuses the rush with which you raced to leave the house. The hurrying around and frantic preparations give way to a purposeful journey during which you can talk or sing.

FINDING OUT

Primary schools have individual ways of receiving new pupils, but there is usually some form of visit beforehand which is very helpful. In choosing the school you will have had a chance to look around yourself and ask questions. If you did not ask them all then, do so now. New parents are expected to want information about the school. It is often more difficult to get these answers later in the year.

Each school will have a booklet describing itself, but see pages 142 to 145 for what to ask and what certain terms mean.

PLAY IS WORK

You will know from the pre-school years how much your child has learned and discovered for herself through play. Play is the child's work and way of finding out. At school, in the reception class her teacher will arrange many activities in the form of games. If you

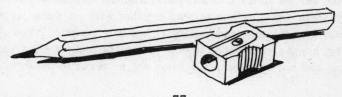

anxiously question your child after school with 'what did you learn today?' or 'what work did you do?' you are most likely to hear 'nothing'. Playing and learning are indistinguishable so you might hear 'just played around'. Keep up this line of questioning and your relaxed, happy pupil might begin to think that she should be doing something else at school called learning. She may worry for no reason.

A NEW WORLD

The bewildering, crowded place called school with its rules – some school rules, others enforced by children in the playground – takes some getting used to. Rather like immigrating to a new land, your child must accommodate herself to a new system, new food, and new people. This takes no time at all for one child, or a couple of terms for another. During this period of adjustment your child's learning may seem slightly set back for a while. Her physical routine may also be new. Perhaps lunch is later than it used to be and she becomes tired and hungry? Girls especially will occasionally not use the toilet at school, and hang on until they get home. Adjustments are made in time by all children, but during this time each child needs a little extra love and support at home. A child learns best when her social life is sorted out and she can turn her attention away from how to manage, to concentrate fully on new skills.

Now is the time to re-read all her favourite books with her. Without any strain, enjoying the ones she already knows can reinforce her confidence and she can try out any new reading skills safely with you. If she brings home word cards that her teachers would like her to learn to recognize, help her to become familiar with them, but continue to read together with emphasis on the meaning of the text, and looking at words in context. When she brings home a school book to read you will be lucky if it is a 'real' book, and not a reader. A real book will be closer to the form of reading you have been doing with your child, and she will not be tempted to see school reading as different from home reading.

It is not true to say that every school reading scheme is unsatisfactory, for publishers have recognized the importance of good writing, and in some cases have commissioned well-known children's authors to do a series. But, for a school to invest in a reading scheme is a costly business, and schemes bought once tend to stay around in school for years. Many outdated schemes prove boring for the child and especially so for the adult. Contrast the book brought home from school with those you have been reading with your child. Does it delight eye, ear and heart? Is it too easy or hard for your child? A simple test of difficulty is to measure how often your child sticks at a word she cannot guess or make out. Is this one in every five? Six?

STRATEGY

It is best not to go rushing in to your child's new teacher with a barrage of complaints, insisting that your genius is above this boring book. Try to assess the teacher's intention. In a class of 25 children, she will be trying to find out what they know, and what they can do in the first weeks. Her plan may be to let your child go on to free choice once she has 'got through' this book or level. If so, it is hardly worth making a fuss. Instead help your child to get past this small hurdle and on to a better range of books.

On the other hand, these books could prove a problem because:

- they are too difficult for your child and she is beginning to think she can't read, or
- she seems stuck on these forever . . . but can read or almost read the books you have been reading together.

You would probably want a friendly word with the teacher if this is the case.

Undemanding children go unnoticed in a new group. Your child's teacher will have to give her time and attention to those who seem to need it most. If your child seems to be managing fine, takes home the reader without murmur and attempts to read it politely when asked, the teacher may not have the time to discover that this child needs different reading material. Usually, a reception class teacher will be helped by knowing about your child, and will provide some worthwhile books for you and your child to share. She will probably be pleased that you are taking an interest and helping your child.

A BRICK WALL

Your efforts may come up against a brick wall – usually taking the form of . . . 'This is how we do it here . . .' or 'We like this scheme because it enables us to measure the child's progress' or, worst of all, 'It does not help if parents carry out something different at home.' If this happens you simply have to carry on reading with your child as before, but widening the range of books as she matures. Help with anything the teacher sends home, but do not spend too long on it. Don't let your disapproval be seen by your child, and try to be positive about other aspects of the teacher's work. Are there other ways in which you can support this teacher? Help with a session of craft? Mend the books in the classroom? Go on an outing? If you can establish a relaxed relationship with the teacher in some area other than reading, she may feel less criticized or threatened by your intervention in reading.

Gradually you can ease into a more co-operative situation. Your child will be pleased to find you get on well with her teacher. The teacher may show more interest in the child and discover more about her reading with time. But, if there is no improvement in the reading material your 5-year-old is given, you will have to make up for this in your reading with her at home.

USE WRITING

Remember that writing is a powerful strand of literacy. Reading is the retrieval of meaning; writing records meaning. Why not record your child's words in writing, let her read them, and even write them out beneath yours, herself? This way you further her reading and writing with no conflict about the reading book. Read Share the importance of writing on page 69 and Let's use writing on pages 70–72. Practising writing on page 91 will give you more on the technique of forming the letters and training the hand.

TOO DEPENDENT?

Schools expect children to be reading independently by the time they are about 7 years old. Your aims, then, over the first two years of school life will take this into account. There is much to be said for bringing children to independent reading quickly. This can prevent readers becoming bored. Endless repetition is fun for under-fives, but fives want more from stories. You will want to reach the stage where you are sharing books as equal partners. Your role should be to support your child as she tries increasingly to take over for herself.

If learning to read takes a very long time, a new reader could become too dependent on the adult and this dependency can increase rather than decrease. This can happen when the child is corrected very often and does not have the habit of trying the difficult word for herself. She will reach a sticking point and stop, waiting for you to say the word. She may concentrate on getting the words right and not hold the story in her mind due to all the interruptions.

Keep the sense uppermost, and encourage the child to guess what the word might be. A child who is told to 'get that page word-perfect' before she can turn over must re-read the same page endlessly and certainly joylessly. There is no reason to make sense of it, no exciting story to discover, in fact, no apparent purpose. The child may become passive. More and more she thinks she cannot do this and you will give her the word. She may become scared to try for herself for fear of making a mistake if she has been corrected too much and too severely. She needs to know that mistakes don't matter but that the sense of the story does.

THE STORY IS VITAL

You want to become the child's partner in enjoyment, rather than always leading the way. Keep the adventure. Choose books carefully and appropriately. Don't interrupt a good story to point out special facts about the text. Do discuss the words used where they are interesting or unknown, but do this briefly at a point where it does not spoil the flow of the story. Some children become impatient and are prepared to leave out a few words they don't know rather as adults do in silent reading.

TOO MUCH TECHNIQUE?

- If we overdo the instructions, the child focuses on these in a narrow concentration on technique. She loses sight of the purpose of reading – the story. Without meaning she cannot get it right. She reads a word at a time.
- Try to encourage her to read chunks of words at a time. 'Around the corner' or 'Under the tables' go together easily, allowing her to use the patterns of the language to help her.

KEEP READING ALOUD

Continue to read to a new reader. She may find reading very tiring but still needs good stories to extend her reading and language skills. A 5-year-old likes action. She may be able to listen to a story way above her reading capacity and her spoken vocabulary will be shooting ahead. Listening to you read will help her reading as the language patterns settle in her unconscious for later recall. You are also keeping the purpose of reading before her as a clear-cut goal.

BOOKS WITH NATURAL USE OF LANGUAGE

Learning to write, read and spell means knowing about patterns of strings of letters and groups of words. This helps a child read as she anticipates meaning. In a primer prepared solely with phonics in mind, meaning may be absent. There will be few clues that normal language patterns offer. Words may be grouped unnaturally. Make sure that a child gets to tackle a text with natural sounding language.

UNDERSTANDING CONTENT

Imagine yourself faced with a scientific textbook on a subject about which you know little or nothing. It may be in English, but you simply cannot read it because you don't understand it. This is not because you cannot recognize sounds, but because you cannot make head or tail of the meaning. You know the code but, despite this, meaning eludes you. This is also true if you don't know the language. You may know the letters and sounds but you are unable to unlock the meaning of the print. In the very early stages children should only read what they can understand.

POSSESSING THE LANGUAGE

For a child who does not yet use the language with confidence, teaching her to read puts the cart before the horse. Talking and reading to her will help her come to 'possess' the language, making it her own natural form of expression. This will prepare her for reading. Talking about the pictures makes language more specific. Answering questions and not 'talking down' to a child helps to enlarge her use of the language. Value her efforts and listen carefully to her re-telling of an event or story, no matter how wandering or hesitant.

- Some children copy a monotonous reading style they hear other children use at school, thinking that this is what is expected of them. Try to ease back into natural rhythm and expression. A child may be concentrating on getting each word right or even syllable. It is a positive step when she begins grouping words together in chunks of text.
- On television, the advertisements feature catchy jingles or phrases which you can play with. Your child may be very familiar with some of them. Practise reading them if they appear on screen, but if they are only heard on the radio, write them out for her to look at. Use songs she knows and write out the words for her. She will be recognizing whole phrases this way. Show her how she can recognize whole phrases in her book too.
- Flash cards with individual words only make this situation worse. The words are seen on their own, out of context. If you would like to use flash cards, write out a complete phrase using the little words that children often stick on.
- Turn a new book into a familiar one by reading it to your child first. When it is her turn, remind her how the story goes by saying 'You remember how it goes.' Talk about what will happen next, prediction and anticipation are helpful clues.
- Some children don't go through all the stages of learning their ABC and sounds but can read. Others know letters and sounds

but can't read. Tailor your activities to your child's needs. If you can avoid the idea that reading is difficult or complicated and concentrate on expecting success, your child will have an easier time. Parents teach best in their natural parenting style. There is no need to try to become a teacher.

At home, you will by now have moved from reading with your child on your lap to sitting side by side, sharing the book. Occasionally you may like to read together in unison, at other times you may each read some of the text to each other. Let your child read the familiar phrases, or the repeated lines where she can be sure of success. It is important that she does not get a sense of failure. Locked away in the print is a message. The child has some of the keys to get it, but she may not have them all yet.

'BUT SHE IS ONLY GUESSING . . .'

Parents occasionally say this when they think that their child ought to be tackling unknown words with specially taught skills. If they were taught phonics, they tend to wonder why the child is not sounding out the letters and blending them as they were made to do.

Phonics, though useful, can only be one of several ways in which we puzzle out meaning from print. English does not lend itself to this method because around 40 per cent of the language does not fit into phonic rules, it is irregular.

Take the letters 'h o' for example. Here are a few ways that these two letters can sound:

house	horse	hood
hoist	hook	holy
hoe	hour	holly
hoot	hound	hole
hot	hooligan	hoarse
how	honest	

When tackling print, your child will be using a group of cues:

- Semantic cues which draw on her knowledge of words.
- Syntactic cues which draw on her knowledge of the context and pattern of the spoken language.
- Predictions, which she can check by using phonic cues.

She might also recall the shape of words from memory.

The letters are not the only clues, though. How about the punctuation marks and the spaces between words and lines? If you see a question mark at the end of a sentence beginning 'W... is the time?' you will know the first word. Are you guessing?

If your child reads 'Once .... there ...', she will know the conventions of story-telling well enough to supply these words.

In a sentence such as 'Mary was afraid that her mother would be angry because she had f........ to buy milk' she can assume the word is 'forgotten'. If she is hesitantly reading one word at a time, her eye will not be so likely to skim to the end of the line and pick up the clues. Instead she will see the long word and may stick. Being confident enough to scan the line, and see groups of words in chunks, will help your child to deduce what the word might be. If she reaches the end of the sentence and the word she supplied does not make sense, she is likely to spot it herself.

Adults do this all the time. Try reading this piece from a newspaper article:

'He points ... that playworkers have little .. ... way .f job specifi.. ...., prospects, status, p.. and especially training. He wants to ... a recognized academic qu............ and the sort .. recognition .. their w..k that youth w..k... or t..ch..s get.'

You will have found from this that you try to unlock meaning from these lines, using your knowledge of the language, and the layout of the letters and lines.

Help a child to concentrate on meaning and you are not likely to hear 'He jumped on his house and rode away'.

A GOOD TEXT CAN TEACH

For an early reader, a well-written text will lead her to the right word through rhyme and repetition, without being meaningless.

We are told in *Arthur's Uncle* by Kit Wright that Arthur's uncle was a long, thin, skinny man, thin as string and tall as a tree. So what might the missing word be here?

'When you laid out Arthur's Uncle flat,
    It was miles from his boots to his ...'

If I read these next two lines out loud to you, would you remember the last word next time we came to it?

'Then Arthur's Uncle bent in half
    And unwound himself like a long thin scarf!'

Your child remembers the word because she has begged you to read this book umpteen times. She sees the 's' coming and she knows it is 'scarf' through using a combination of factors. Most importantly she 'knows' she is reading. Her confidence builds in precisely this way.

So a good text actually helps the reader read.

A good story makes the reader want to read, to turn over the page and find out what comes next, to discover meaning in print for herself. A well-crafted text can be a masterpiece of writing in which the author gives delight, humour and suspense using very few words. These words are arranged in such a way that the reading seems effortless and natural. These are the books to look for.

Sentences such as the old-fashioned 'Come John come, come and see' offer none of these delights.

HOW CAN I ASSESS PROGRESS?

Your child's progress will be apparent not because she is now reading book two or three of a scheme, but because she makes sense from print.

- How successful is she in using cues to determine meaning?
- Does she manage some but not all of these strategies?
- Can she tell you about what she has just read?
- Will she pick up a book of her own accord and try to read it?
- Does she see herself as a reader?
- Does she read a word at a time or does she read groups of words?
- Does she remember the text of a favourite book and 'read' it back to you?
- Can she recognize any of the words in that text when seen elsewhere?
- Does she look at public print and say 'I know what that says' or does she still need to ask you 'What does that say?'

If you are reading regularly together you will know when she starts to read in unison, or takes over from you now and again. You will know when she points to a word and says that she knows what it means. You won't need reading tests, or books of graded levels to tell you when your child is reading for herself – the excitement and sense of achievement are so evident. She will progress in her own time and not in relation to other children. If your child shows none of these signs and is very reluctant to look at books you will know that she is not becoming a reader. Read the sections at the start of this book and try to help her become 'Hooked on books'.

Did all the children you know begin to talk at the same age? They all talk in the end. Children can come to reading at different ages and catch up remarkably quickly provided that they have an idea of the purpose of reading and the confidence to try it for themselves.

The story of reading chart on p.152 shows the various stages of progress, though you will notice they have not been grouped by age.

READING WITH DAD

There are more boys than girls in remedial classes. Could this be linked to the fact that many fathers spend their time with their sons playing football or taking them on outings? These are valuable pursuits of course, but, unwittingly, a father may give the impression that reading is somehow unmanly.

Most primary teachers are women, and Mum may be the person he reads with at home, so your son may subconsciously perceive reading as less than macho.

This is easily corrected once you are aware of it. I mention it here simply as a reminder. Dads or other male relatives may be wonderful story-tellers once they get going, and the warmth and security found in a great bear hug will make story-time special.

HOW LONG SHOULD I CONTINUE TO READ TO MY CHILD?

Once a child can read, we find ourselves listening to her read to us more often than not. Then the child moves on to silent reading, perhaps in bed at night after we have said goodnight. Some parents think that if they read aloud to a child who can read they are somehow making the child lazy. But think how adults enjoy stories on the radio and you will know that there is no age at which people don't need to be read to.

You may not need to read aloud to this child every night, but there are times when the child is tired and overworked, when reading for school work has demanded all her energy. How marvellous then to let her sink back onto the pillow while you embark on a series, such as Susan Cooper's *The Dark is Rising* (Bodley Head, 1984). Once past the present hump this child will eagerly continue the series for herself. You will know the characters and be able to ask what is happening. In this way a child of 10 or 11, working hard on 'projects' and doing mostly reference reading, will not lose out on fiction.

If your child can read but doesn't, there is no easier way to get her hooked on books again than by choosing a riveting read and reading to her. Children who are avid readers may, for various reasons, slip into a period of several months of new experiences so absorbing that they forget about reading. Never nag, for this child has a good attitude to books, and you do not want to change that. Spend a little time choosing a good read-aloud (consider *The Read Aloud Handbook* by Jim Trelease, Penguin, 1984) or ask a librarian, and read to your child.

Extend a child's reading experience by reading aloud. You may be tackling a book together which she may not cope with alone.

GAMES

Practising writing

Children do not have to be working at writing. Playing around with a pencil and paper is interesting enough on its own. The child will discover some of the different marks she can make on the paper by experimenting. Some children enjoy puncturing the paper with forceful dots, others will latch on to one shape and repeat it all over the page. Try to show your child from the start how to hold the pencil correctly, between thumb and forefinger, resting on the third finger.

Squiggles are more free-flowing when made with a brush and paint. Try squiggling together in finger paint (see the recipe for finger paint on page 33). Show your child a few of these patterns and allow a few weeks play with pattern if she seems interested. The patterns can be left as they are or coloured in to form other shapes. The identical pattern can be drawn upside down above the first if you turn the paper around.

When the child shows an interest in letters and is recognizing them in public print and in books and writing, she may ask you to show her how to make them. You can then introduce them in shape families as shown in the diagram opposite.

Some children never learn to write this way. They may ask you to write out their own words beneath a picture, or a story, and then copy your writing for themselves. They may already know how to write their name from seeing it written for them. Try to interest your child and follow her lead. Remember you can write

- On steamy windows
- On sand with a stick or finger
- With a sharp object on waxed paper

- With paint and brush
- With finger paint and fingers or toes
- With water on rock, asphalt or stone paths
- With many different types of crayons and felt-tip pens/markers
- On various types of paper.

Pencils do give a great deal of control, but there are moments when the freedom of a big brushstroke is thrilling.

Give your child plenty of time to play and experiment with writing/scribbling without giving any instruction. Keep paper and pencil handy and offer it when you both have to wait at the doctor's or at restless moments when you're not at home with toys. At home keep a range of papers, crayons, paints.

Writing play

Certain recurring patterns are found in the formation of letters. Copying patterns helps with manual control - doing it from left to right helps create this habit. Let your child play with squiggles.

Letters are grouped in 'shape families' and the easiest to start with are:

i l u y j

then:

r n m h b p k

while these go together . . .

c a d g q o e

all have straight lines in them

v w x z

are left over.

t f s

For older children – 5 and over only: lines show where the letters are placed.

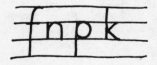

Left-handers should grip the pencil, crayon or whatever about 4 cm (1½ in) from the point so that they can see what they are writing. Place the paper slightly to the left of centre of their bodies and either slant it slightly to the right or line it up against the edge of the table.

Form the letters in this direction:

a b c d e f g h i j k l m n
o p q r s t u v w x y z

Which is the odd one out?

key   kettle   spoon

How many things can you find that start with 's'?

sink   Simon   Susan   sock   spoon   scissors   snake

Early writing

Five to six

- Make a rag book for a baby by using non-toxic fabric paint and a laundry marker to write the words. Your six-year-old will love to do this. The fabric pages can be cut with pinking shears. Keep pictures very simple, for example a ball on one page, a duck on another.

- Write a list of the birds you see feeding at your bird table or nut net. (These are available in pet shops and some supermarkets). Your child can make a mark against the appropriate bird name whenever you receive a visit from that bird.

- Give home-made gifts and have your child write 'With love from . . .'. They will be enthusiastic makers of cards and gift tags which can be made from stiff card, such as the sheets found inside new shirts, or packs of tights.
- Think of three wishes, draw a picture and write beneath something about each wish.
- Make a series of drawings illustrating a story. Write beneath simple captions in the child's own words.

Secret writing

If your child writes a message in milk or orange juice, with a sharp quill-like object, it will become invisible when dry. When the message is held near a *gentle* heat source, such as a light bulb or candle, it becomes visible. An adult should help with the second step.

Another form of secret writing is made using a white wax crayon on white paper. This, too, is invisible. But, when a wash of colour, dye, watercolour paint, or diluted ink is washed over it, the waxed area stays white.

How your new reader can help you

Examining the ingredients in the groceries you buy? If you read the labels, your six-year-old can be a great help in examining everything you buy for artificial colouring or whatever you are on the lookout for. Show her where the list is, and for the first few times show her the words you are looking for, then she will do the job for you.

Which way?

Instructions, signs and arrows can all be deciphered by your child. This side up, Exit, Turn to open, Cut here, Ladies, Gents toilet, No right turn.

When and Where?

Date stamps, Eat by . . . Sell by . . . Best before . . .
On public transport have her look for the signs you need, which line? Which stop? Where do we change? Where are we now? How many stops are there until we arrive?

97

USE YOUR CHILD AS A SCRIBE

- Encourage your child to help with shopping lists. She can make the list and tick off the items as you find them.
- Messages for members of the family are important and a child of 5 or 6 likes to be entrusted with some worthwhile job, not fobbed off with something she considers babyish. She can write out messages carefully and stick them up on the fridge or wherever your family put them. This child will also help when you require a notice telling the family to keep off a dish you have made for expected guests, or prepared for tomorrow. Faced with this suggestion, one child put a skull and crossbones on her sign and wrote POISON beneath!
- 'I must not forget' notices are perfect to do, because they lend themselves to lurid squiggles with fluorescent markers or highlighters, and every five- or six-year-old would like to use these, like her parents do for 'work'.
- If you make jam, have your child make decorated labels. This keeps her safely out of the way of the boiling pot.

- An important chart is an assignment that proves the worth of your child's effort. There can be a chart showing what to take to school on which day. Write out the days of the week and let your child draw or write (or both) the gear she must remember on Monday etc. Is it P E kit today? Swimming?
- For keen gardeners a chart of chores is practical and can be adorned with drawings of flowers - or slugs! List when you sowed vegetable and flower seeds. Your child can copy the writing from seed packets and help to check on plants' progress.

Other ideas for charts can be drawn from your busy life. If you share taking children to school with another family do a chart of who is fetching when.

Children learn by doing, not being told. What better way to understand the importance and usefulness of writing, and of course reading, than helping the family?

HE ISN'T READING YET

If as your child approaches seven, he is not showing signs of moving to independent reading, he may need a little burst of help to learn to read. Some experts consider that for a child under 7, remedial classes are no solution. They maintain that either the child can read, or he cannot. If the latter is true, then he needs to be taught to read.

'Hospitalizing' the child by removing him from the class is not the answer, they believe. Nor is giving him more of what he has shown he cannot do, going to turn him into a reader. Whatever action you take it is important to reinforce the child's confidence. If he thinks he has become a special case, he might truly believe that he cannot overcome the difficulties. He may believe there is a reason for this, such as a physical illness. Adults, too, seem grateful to believe that there is a defect responsible for his inability to read.

You will, of course, have had all basic vital checks made on your child's health. If there were any permanent conditions they would show up in other areas of life.

ANY OTHER PROBLEMS?

Ask yourself whether the child has other problems on his mind. Anything that represents an upheaval in his life, emotionally or physically, may have upset him. What is his general adjustment to school? How is he coping in other fields? If he shows intelligence in every other field and there is a discrepancy between his ability in general, and his failure to read, the cause may be found now. Have a word with the teacher and try to see his reading in a wider context.

Confidence

If you find that school is making this child feel inadequate you will need to build confidence at home. If the child is confused by too many instructions, he may have lost sight of reading as he tries to carry out all the instructions he has been given. A more relaxed approach could work. Make sure he knows reading is for pleasure and reinstate the story as the most important goal of reading.

MAKE HIM FEEL SECURE

A child fearful of making mistakes may decide not to take risks so reads a word at a time very hesitantly. You will try to help this child to take chances, guess from the meaning of the sentence, and trust himself. He can only do this when he is not constantly corrected. Let him read to the end of the sentence and see whether or not he realizes the mistake. For this child, the meaning may not be helping him, because he is nervously concentrating on getting individual words right. Remind him of the sense of what he is reading, talk about what has happened and what might come next in the story. Encourage him to try to keep in mind the story as he reads.

If he substitutes a word that still makes sense, he is doing fine. Absolute accuracy is not necessary, reading for meaning is. Do remember that even the most fluent adult readers make mistakes when reading aloud.

HE READS, BUT NOT ALOUD

Some children can extract meaning from print, but do not like reading aloud.

Talk to this child about what he has been reading. If he has understood his story, try to reinforce his confidence and share the interest of the story in informal chat.

- Read aloud yourself to all seven-year-olds, no matter how well they read.

EXTRA READING CLASSES?

If the school suggests taking him out of class for extra help with reading, find out what form this will take. If he is going to hate this, because he is made to seem different from his friends, or because he is forced to do more of something he dislikes or cannot do, he may build up a deep-seated dislike of reading. I have heard children in a 'remedial group' being told to sit up and read that page word perfect before they can go on to the next. This would turn off even the most enthusiastic child. In hesitant readers it breeds sulky resentment.

If, however, the help offered is caring, friendly and will increase exposure to stories, ask how you can help at home. Perhaps books will be sent home for you to share. A key factor is writing. Will this be used to help his reading? At home you can write out his own words to textless picture books, or accounts of an adventure he has had, and have him write it, read it, and possibly tape it.

Any old photo albums about? Use photographs of an event to jog his memory and write out his account of that. Look through the suggestions in this book on writing activities and try a few if he likes the idea.

- Foster imagination: listen to music and think of words to describe it. Paint or write them out in suitable colours. Write complete sentences wherever possible.
- To remind your child how reading is part of our everyday life, use TV timetables together, and teach him to look up programme schedules.
- Does he have a favourite sport? Follow reports about the sport or team in the press.
- Have him help read recipes out to you, while making something he likes together. (He might make up a packet mix reading the instructions for himself.)
- Bought a new gadget for home or garden? Let him help with the instruction leaflet.

DR WHO?

A 7-year-old wants to be like his mates. If they are all into football, most of the class will be too. Interests widen dramatically now and your seven-year-old son or daughter may be gaining skills in sports or dancing at an amazing speed. If your child is struggling with reading, find out if there are some popular books being read by the faster readers in the class. If Paddington or Clever Polly are doing the rounds it is important that the slower reader experiences these books in order to have the chance to talk the same language as those children who may refer to these stories. Read them aloud to your child. This gives a sense of belonging to the group. It is the sort of 'knowing' that counts in the playground.

Children talk about TV programmes and often tease those who don't know what they mean. You might read some of the books that accompany these children's TV programmes too. One child will love books about an interest like ballet or football, another dislikes them because he thinks he knows about that, and wants something totally new. Put time and effort into choosing a tempting range of books to read to and with your child. They want to be like their friends now.

Above all make it clear that you have every confidence that he will be able to read for himself soon. To succeed, the child must know that you believe in him. He must trust and like his teacher. If you and the teacher agree on how to help him and work together towards this, he will feel supported.

If books have become a subject of friction or argument in any way, leave them for a while. Instead, use opportunities for reading in everyday life, and, of course, as much writing as you can, especially of the child's own descriptions of events.

5

· · · · ·

Eight and Over

As school work demands more reading for information, story reading for information, story reading may decrease. Teachers and parents alike assume the child can read and is reading so they may take less interest.

Hunting for material for school projects leads the child to learn to skim through information books looking for the piece of information he needs. Some children need help to learn how to do this. Looking up in an index is simple when you know how, daunting when you don't.

HUNGRY FOR FACTS

There are various elements to your child's reading at this stage. Most obvious of course will be a search for facts. Not only related to school work, but perhaps your child is fascinated by space travel or football, and amasses amazing amounts of detail on his subject. Games with other children often centre around 'trump cards' in which details of ships or, say, aircraft are used to play a complex game. Your role, as ever, is to help with a selection of books.

Helping to find a range that fills the needs of these voracious fact-gatherers means regular visits to the library. One week it may be 'which is the longest river?', the next, 'how do pianos work'? Very few home libraries can cover every aspect of an eight-year-old's curiosity . . . but a few good reference books and your own collection, based on your interests, will be put to good use.

DON'T NEGLECT FICTION

However, this search for facts, and our assumption that eight-year-olds are reading, leads both parents and teachers frequently to neglect fiction now. Many children talk of finding fairy tales 'boring', stories 'babyish' and demonstrate shorter spans of concentration than before.

TV AND CONCENTRATION

They are now watching various fascinating programmes regularly on television, and, apart from children's programmes, they will be enjoying wildlife, new inventions, sport and the development of aircraft, to name a few. These are all offering entertainment and facts packed into short bursts of time. They require little or no active effort on the child's part, and, in a sense, he is not developing an ability to concentrate for longer periods in a sustained effort.

SATISFYING SERIES

It is vital to keep feeding this child fiction. This can only be successful if the books are chosen with care and suited to the child – the golden rule at any age. As he moves from 8 to 9, the reader sees new worlds opening up for him and has a healthy disdain for 'childish' things. By 9 children have developed a sensitivity to social behaviour and are very conscious of the subtleties of the personalities in his class. Bullies and victims, showoffs and teacher's pets are all revealed to him as he has become very perceptive. He will want to read adventure books, short novels that explore what seems to be a slightly older world than his own. The struggles these characters endure and overcome will help him in his effort to gain a perspective on what he sees lying ahead.

LEGEND AND MYTH – BIBLE AND FOLK TALES

Yes, some stories are too babyish for him. But for generations tales of legendary heroes and villains; adversity and triumph; tests and wisdom have been passed down. Without these he is deprived of a background and the knowledge he needs to make sense of our world.

Look at legend and myth, share tales from the Bible. Consider the stories of other cultures. Here is common ground between adult and child; the stories are part of the parent's childhood too. These tales used to be passed down in an oral tradition of story-telling, they were always shared by generations and are universal. References to them will be dotted about in your child's later reading. There will be phrases in everyday language and proverbs made clear by this knowledge of a heritage.

Unresolved fears can be overcome as stories focus and order the conflicting chaos of our inner emotions. Heroes struggle and triumph, victims are rescued and dragons slain, all symbols of the struggles of real life.

Bible tales and folk tales of other cultures provide a rich source of reading which enables us to develop roots and understanding. Tolerance and a broader view come from reading about other lands and peoples. Discussing the issues raised in a story offers a parent an opportunity to share a debate with a child without seeming to be lecturing him.

Silent sustained reading needs developing now if reading is not to be mainly skimming and short bursts of fact-finding. With a little thought and occasionally reading aloud to your child, you can start a series, or a craze for one particular author. The child, once hooked, will carry on.

HELP WITH FACT-FINDING

You will also need to help with reference books. Many information books prepared for children prove too superficial, and after the initial glossy presentation do not hold enough depth.

The Hutchinson *Twentieth Century Encyclopaedia* and Macmillan's *Children's Encyclopaedia* form a good basis to a collection of reference books. The Pears *Junior Cyclopaedia* is recommended by some, though we have always used the adult version. A good atlas, a basic dictionary, and books of your choice on modern history answer many questions.

HANDLE WITH CARE AND TACT – 9 TOWARDS 11

Don't overdo books on every interest a child mentions. A burgeoning interest is easily crushed under the weight of a heavy tome which an over-eager adult says 'you must read'.

As the child develops some skill at chess, he may want to find out more about advanced moves. He may not want to read a huge book on the history of the game and the moves of each piece right away.

A general collection of books at home can be augmented by the library. Only buy a specialized book when the need for it is clear and you are satisfied that the book you are considering is neither too superficial nor dauntingly dull. Many glossy productions look exciting but contain little. Is the book by one author or is it a compilation with many contributors? Some compilations are successful, but they may lack a direct 'voice', that of an author passionate about this subject.

It is sometimes more successful to offer several books on a subject, from the library. Valuable material can be gained from each. Your child can learn to sift facts and form an opinion when he is offered varied views on one event. Let the child hunt for information as he needs it. In the search for something he really wants to know, a child will pursue the subject like a sleuth and will prefer adult books. You can help your child in the following ways:

- Help in finding the relevant books.
- Show the reader how to find the material he needs in the book.
- Chat about the subject and help to select what he needs, so that he does not copy indiscriminately from the text.
- Ask 'What is needed here? What are the most important elements? What is relevant and useful?'
- Encourage the child to *read, discuss, select* and then *write* down points.
- Show the child how to assess the content. Is the book biased? Is there another viewpoint? Has the historical perspective changed?

IS THIS BOOK OFFENSIVE?

Books cause a reaction in us because of attitudes they display, or the way certain issues are handled. Books are written, after all, by individuals and we don't expect to agree with everyone on any given subject.

Assess the books yourself if your child is young and you know the book deals with a subject on which you hold strong views. Teach a child to judge for himself as he reads – developing a critical sense is what makes a real reader of him. Is there gratuitous violence? Are sexist or racist ideas expressed?

Children are made aware of these issues in primary schools today. However, they often misunderstand or misinterpret material and you may need to explain. I have heard children criticizing protest songs of the sixties (which they learned to sing at school in the eighties) because they had missed the point of the protest and thought the song espoused the concept it existed to expose. (The

song *Little Boxes* required a great deal of explaining to children who thought it advocated putting people into little boxes.)

Naturally we want to avoid deeply offensive material, but, going to extremes in this leaves the reader with only 'sanitized' books. Books that avoid offending cat lovers, ecologists and anti-sexist campaigners all rolled into one are rare indeed. Better to offer a variety of opinion and make up one's own mind than read pasteurized books devoid of all opinion. The author's view penetrates all writing, however subtle or obvious – so this cannot be avoided. In fact this 'point of view' of the author, this way of viewing the world, is what makes a particular book interesting.

SEX AND VIOLENCE

The ugly aspects of society are displayed in detail on TV. Children no longer have to sneak a sexy book under the bedcovers or desk lid – they can see it all on the screen. So, banning books that are 'too sexy' is useless.

Rather than 'forbidding' a book, which only serves to make it more tempting, offer a wide selection of books you do approve of, leaving it open to the child to form his own opinion of each. Some books deal in particular with war, some deal with violence and cause the reader to feel a revulsion for it, moving him to respond to mindless acts like these with horror. Words well used are powerful. Have books on your side in a debate you care about.

Children seem eager to read about what lies ahead for them as they mature – so they choose to read about aspects of life they have yet to experience. They may be fascinated by a teenage love story, while still young enough to 'hate' the opposite sex. They see themselves as about to enter this phase and part of the preparation is reading about it. Teenagers are being catered for by a greater number of publishers than ever before. However, your child may simply prefer to go straight on to adult books after 12 or 13.

Search your own book shelves and memory to find a wide range of novels that handle relationships sensitively so that your child can learn of them gracefully. Sooner or later young people will form new relationships themselves and so, naturally, they are keen to read about love.

In the same way, although you will have talked together about the changes that growing up brings, you can also let books do the talking if you feel the author has something to say that is worthwhile. If you offer a wide selection now, it may prevent a slide into 'trash' or surreptitious reading, in the same way, as many people believe, offering their children a glass of wine with special meals makes it less likely that they will seek out alcohol as a forbidden fruit and drink to excess.

FUN WITH BOOKS

Comparing illustrators

Look at different versions of a classic, such as *Alice in Wonderland* or *Peter Pan*, or even nursery rhymes. Discuss the illustrator's work. Which do you prefer? Why? Is a certain style more appropriate? Talk about the mood, style and technique of the pictures.

GAMES

Make your own stories

1 Tape a story with simulated sound effects.
2 Draw a strip illustration of the main action of the story.
3 Using a felt-covered board, arrange characters in scenes from the story. The characters will stick in position if they are felt- or velcro-backed. Cut out pictures from magazines or draw your own.
4 Use finger puppets or glove puppets to make up a story for a younger child.

Compare the book and the film/video

Perhaps you have taken your child to see the film versions of the books *101 Dalmatians* or *Charlie and the Chocolate Factory*. Talk about the differences between the film and book versions. Was the film as the child had imagined it would be? What can you do in a book that you cannot do in a film? Does the book allow you to use your own imagination?

Series quiz

If children are hooked on a series of books, their friends probably are too. A rainy day quiz can be devised by them based on the books. Each sets questions for the other.

Book reviews

- If you share a book together after having seen it reviewed, compare your opinion of it with that of the reviewer. The child has a chance to express his views and develop a critical sense.

- Writing a straight book review is seen by most children as a chore, but chatting about your viewpoint seems so adult. It will help you to know more about the child's taste when looking for the next book to read.

There is a list on page 149 of publications containing reviews of children's books. Your local library or bookshop should be able to help supply one.

- The back cover of the book may quote extracts from reviews. Does your child agree with these?

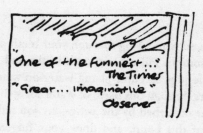

RECORDING A STORY ON TAPE

Go for realistic background noises, which children love to make. If you can record the real sound of the sea for your story, it will give an authentic touch. If not, it is such fun to simulate the crash, roar, gurgles and retreat of the waves over the pebbles on the beach. Talk about the sounds before you start and let the children recall any particular sounds that form part of this soundscape.

- Whistling and whooshing through your teeth provides a variety of useful sounds. Fill a basin with water and pour water into it with little jugs or cups, giving water-on-water sounds. Draw your fingers through this basin of water for swirling water noise. For pebbles disturbed by the waves, lay foil milk bottle tops on the floor of this basin, and draw your fingers through them. Squirter bottles can be useful (if messy) and the plug hole in the bath can offer up gurgles and bubbles.
- Crunch cellophane or crunch salt for footsteps in the snow. Have a child walk into the room wearing the appropriate shoes for the character in the story who has just 'entered'. Would he or she be wearing high heels, boots, squelching rubber soles? Would he or she be shuffling, stamping or running? The detail of the story can be brought out through these discussions, and the children's vocabulary grows and is used with confidence.
- Fingers tapping or pounding on the table can sound like horses' hooves and even train clickety clacks. Cars can be recorded approaching and going off into the distance. Thunder and rain can be achieved with baking sheets, foil and rice or beans falling

noisily onto these surfaces. Rattle a metal tray for thunder. The base boards of Lego sets, if large enough, will give a thunderous roar if shaken to and fro. The seemingly simple sound of a clock ticking can give heightened suspense to a line like 'he waited for what seemed like ages . . .'

- Wind, whistling and creaking, whining hinges and squeaking gates give realism to haunted houses or ghost stories.
- If your story is about an underwater world speak with your mouth just above the level of water in a bowl and occasionally blow bubbles in the water as you speak.

Older children will sometimes take great interest in making a tape for younger children. In doing this well, they are learning a great deal themselves. It is a theatrical production but since mistakes are so easily erased there is little fear of failure.

Remember:
Don't have your mouth too close to the microphone.
Turn your head away when you want the voice to seem far away, or shouting from a distance.

To edit in pre-recorded sound effects, it is necessary to have two tape recorders. Can you beg or borrow a second machine?

Practise the different characters' voices before beginning and try to leave a tiny pause between the end of the speech and the narrator's words such as 'he said':

'I'm rushing down to the station', he said breathlessly.

Here you will want to read the line first, in order to know that it must be delivered breathlessly, and it will help the clarity if you pause slightly between the words 'station' and 'he'. If he then runs off you can have a child run into the distance for a second or two.

The most common mistake in reading aloud is reading too fast, so slow down. Finally, do remember that everyone makes mistakes when reading aloud. Go for meaning and expression and don't stop to correct tiny errors that are unimportant to the story.

SQUARE EYES?

If your child is a TV addict you will need to think of ways to use reading and writing skills.

It is difficult to get a TV-addicted child to read and write when his favourite programme is on. If you can discourage indiscriminate watching, and switch off after that programme has ended, you may be able to avoid the child sitting mesmerized through the advertisements and on through the next one.

Are there ways in which you can use this passion to build skills? Can he write down what happened in that programme? Tell him you hate to miss it, but that you want to know what happens. What does he think might happen next? Was today's episode what he had expected? Prediction is a great help in reading. Expressing the events of the episode in clear terms for you will make him get the events in the right sequence, a good editing task.

- What is the difference between writing for television and writing a story? A script uses dialogue. Have him try writing a dialogue between two of his favourite characters. A child of 10 or 11 could flesh out a script with descriptions of the setting and actions, broken into shots.
- For a child who does not want to write it down, talking is an option. Let him tell you about the programme. Ask about it, ask him his opinion and what he thinks might have happened if the story had been different. Try to encourage him to express himself clearly, and keep the story sequence in order. If he will draw a picture of the hero, a line or two of writing may be included beneath the picture or in speech bubbles.
- Can he look up his programme in a TV guide? If you see anything written about this, for example in the *TV Times* or a newspaper, give it to him to read. Perhaps the star of the show is leaving. Occasional reports might appear. Try to use his enthusiasm for

117

this show, rather than denigrate his addiction. It will not make him a better reader to shout 'Switch that thing off and go and read a book' as you hear the theme music wafting through the house yet again.

WRITING

How free is 'free expression'?

Should you correct your child's written work or will this kill his enthusiasm and creative flow? At first the primary aim is for the child to express his thoughts clearly. If you nitpick you will take away his pride in the work, and his train of thought will be lost.

On the other hand if a child of ten is producing written work without punctuation and with poor spelling, a little help is needed.

Some children will come and ask you how to spell a word as they write. They are aware that there is a correct way of writing words, and make an effort to be accurate. Other children become carried away by the narrative, swept along by what they are putting down. They do not stop for anything, and their words flow out like a flood. There is an exciting element in this, a spontaneity that marks this writer.

If you help, do so in a way that does not alter the structure of the child's language. If the child writes well and is confident, a discussion about paragraphs and sentences might well make his work clearer to read. Eight- or nine-year-olds can put their work in order once they understand this idea. Editing is a very adult thing to do. See it as a professional touch rather than correcting. Explain to the child that authors use paragraphs, and look for them in books.

As your child matures, and writing is no longer a new skill, a gentle move towards accuracy means that his efforts can be better understood by others. One of the main reasons for writing is to be read. Allow the flow of ideas to come first, as your child sorts out his ideas and develops his reasoning and descriptive ability. He may like the idea of making rough notes first, and writing up his text from this. If his first draft is fully written out, but contains many mistakes, he may accept some editing suggestions. However, simply copying everything out twice can be deadening, and your child will be asking for your response to his effort of expression when he shows you his work.

- If your first reaction is to point out and correct mistakes, he may be deeply hurt. The content is the most important element. Read it. Discuss it, and then show that if certain mistakes are corrected it helps the reader understand his valued work *which is worth reading.*
- Don't overdo your help. The child will discover for himself through reading and writing the proper way to do things. Children set their sights high. Your help is valuable only when the child is happy to accept it.

If a child between 9 and 10 is still not using punctuation correctly, has he been shown how to? Does he need a gentle reminder? Does he know but get carried away and forget? Discussing this together can put it right in one afternoon, if you have not been regularly nagging him. If necessary, leave the subject alone for a while and come to it freshly some time later.

Spelling a problem? Try to encourage your child to:

- Say the word in his head as he looks at it.
- Write it out or trace it with a finger.
- Look at it and try to notice any special points about it. Does it look the way it sounds?
- Say the parts of it to himself as it looks to him, for instance, 'nec ces sary'.
- Write it out and mark the difficult part with coloured markers or underline the troublesome letters.

119

- Look away from the word and try to imagine it in his head again. Say it to himself as he tries to form a mental picture of it.
- Write it out from memory without looking at the first one.
- Check it. Try again after underlining or colouring the part that was wrong.

Some spellers know that they have got a word wrong, because 'it looks wrong'. They do not know why, however. Others do not know they have made a mistake. For the first groups it is easier, because their doubt will lead them to check, perhaps in a dictionary or by asking how the word is spelled. It is harder to alert those in the second group to spelling if they do not have a mental picture of what the word should look like. Help them to be more observant about little details and shapes within words.

6

. . . . .

Choosing is Everything

TEXTS WITH MEANING

Texts need to fascinate the child. Children want to gain a better understanding of life, of the world we live in, and how to cope with it. They want texts with meaning.

You might think I have stated the obvious. Sadly, many early texts are quite meaningless or boring. There is an assumption that with a few simple words, endless repetition and occasionally the use of the same consonants over and over again in tongue-twisting lines, a child will miraculously learn how to read. No book of this type could make a child love reading for itself.

> Is it here?
> Where is it?
> It is not here.
> Is it there?

There are so many books of exceptional quality available for children, there should be no excuse for offering them dull, mediocre material. We need to provide a wide range of books that stimulate and enrich the imagination, books that feed the soul with literary images of man and nature. Books that bring to life three-dimensional images of people in their struggle to resolve some of life's problems. Wit and humour, sensitivity and poetic vision are all accessible in the rich selection of fiction for children.

However, if you're under five you are totally dependent on your parents, librarian or teacher to offer you books to read. Once at school, a child may be able to choose from a good selection there or at the local library, but, as tastes develop it is more important than ever to make time available to take children to the library or bookshop to choose books.

IMAGINARY PEOPLE

Children learn only gradually that words are symbols for the object they name. At first many cannot grasp this.

It is hard for a young child to realize that words such as 'I' or 'you' or 'Mum' in a story do not refer to her or her parents specifically. This often leads to a situation in which a child finds that saying certain lines, or in fact the story itself, is offensive in some way. It may be that she cannot imagine acting in this manner. Perhaps the child is offended by what the character has to say or do.

Gradually young readers begin to realize by exposure to many stories, that these words and names refer to imaginary people in an imagined setting.

The power to transport the reader into this imagined setting is one of the most potent features of story-telling. Through the language of stories the child's imagination is extended and stimulated. The story evokes a reaction in the child. It is easy to understand how important the choice of reading material is for a particular reader.

If the child is repeatedly faced with stories that disturb or upset her, she may decide that *she dislikes reading for the effect it has on her.*

An adult faced with a book that disturbs, bores or irritates, can simply discard it and take another. When watching a movie or TV we often look away when we don't want to see a certain scene we can anticipate. Children, on the whole, when starting to read are expected to read what they are given.

A VERY SPECIAL BOOK

Many new readers come to reading through a 'breakthrough book' – a book that has proved so attractive to them that they have been irresistibly drawn to it. Repetition has made it come alive for them and they begin to read for themselves through this book. They see the point of making the effort, and become so attracted to a certain book that it comes to represent their breakthrough into independent reading.

Textless books can offer enormous learning opportunities as the 'reader' must supply her own words, and in the telling, makes the tale her own. This way, the well-known story-telling conventions are learned. Knowing how stories 'work' helps all readers predict and anticipate. As the child follows the exploits of the central characters she must keep the episodes in sequence in her mind, she needs to connect one to the other, linking cause and effect. The child feels a sense of ownership as if she has a hand in creating the story as she fleshes it out with detail.

In re-telling, children often memorize what they have decided is the text, and repeat it word perfect for weeks. You might tape record this and write it down. Raymond Briggs' *The Snowman* (Hamish Hamilton, 1978) is excellent for this purpose. By avoiding the spoken word cassette at first (though it is pleasing) you might play the music to the child to add to the mood.

Shirley Hughes' *Up and Up* (Armada Books, 1981) requires many contributions from the reader as she makes her way through the uncertainty of the start, picks up detail, resolves ambiguity, appreciates the irony and navigates through fantasy and reality. Much time will be spent poring over this.

Because of these considerations, the *content* of the book we offer plays an important part in forming the child's attitude to reading. Choosing books for children needs care and sensitivity. Writing books for them even more so. Parents need to seek out caring authors.

Many 'good' books will not be liked by every child, but many titles have proved themselves again and again with generations of children. There is a recent flowering of books for the young and if you have not studied the book scene since your ten-year-old was a toddler you may find it has become even more exciting.

BOOKS WITH SOULS

For under fives especially, there are gems by author/illustrators where the text and pictures harmonize to give a striking result. This small selection shows how books for very young children don't need to be simplistic or condescending. These present complex ideas in clear terms and pure artistry.

The Most Wonderful Egg in the World by Helme Heine (Armada Books, 1985) presents the age-old quarrel about who is the most beautiful, told in 200 words. This is finally happily resolved and friendship triumphs. This book is satisfying emotionally, and the illustrations wonderfully witty. The rivals are hens. One is shown poking her head between her scrawny legs atop a wall. The text reads, 'Stalky had the most beautiful legs'. The king, to whom the contestants go for advice, says, 'It's not how you look but what you do that counts.'

Another masterpiece in 200 words, in clear, large print, is Brian Wildsmith's *What the Moon Saw* (Oxford University Press, 1985). In vivid pictures he presents some contrasting concepts when the sun and the moon talk about what they can see. Beauty and humour make the illustrations stunning as always in this artist's work. There is much to discuss in this book and his versions of the La Fontaine fables.

John Burningham has provided a wealth of excellent titles over the years and we have been enchanted with *Trubloff* (Pan Books, 1972), the mouse that played the balalaika. Our three-year-old had never heard of Eastern Europe, but knew that every mouse she ever saw, be it model, toy or real mouse, was quite definitely Trubloff!

In *Borka, The Adventures of a Goose With no Feathers* (Penguin, 1978), he shows a hapless goose finally ending up at Kew Gardens, where 'the geese did not mind that Borka had no feathers . . . nobody laughed at her grey woollen jersey.' If you are small and worried about being different, you will love Borka. Burningham's books deal with universal themes. Children and adults alike can identify with these books.

In *Not Now Bernard* by David Mckee (Sparrow Books, 1982), Bernard's parents have one answer, even when Bernard tells them a huge monster is about to eat him up, 'Not now Bernard'. There is a smug feeling of I told you so when the monster does eat up Bernard. Readers enjoy the gloating triumph.

Eve Rice's *New Blue Shoes* (Bodley Head, 1977) explores a small girl's gradual assertion of her independence as she chooses blue shoes when her mum had brown in mind. Although Rebecca's mum is embarrassed when Rebecca rejects every pair the 'nice man' brings, she is sensitive when Rebecca needs reassurance about her choice on the way home. The whole story is set against the background of the gentle relationship between Rebecca and her mother.

These authors are a handful whose work for young children is outstanding. Consider other titles by them and consult booklists at the library if you want to see what else an author has produced.

There are established authors of this calibre and there are newcomers too who are very good. To list them all here is not possible but, as a guide, look out for imaginative text and glorious illustrations full of wit and style.

- The books mentioned here deal with issues that concern a child under five as she grapples with life.
- Reading 'books with souls' promises more knowledge and greater clarity in a complex world.
- A good story will be entertaining, have quality illustrations and a satisfying structure.
- Choose books with natural cadences and language patterns,

rather than stilted, contrived sentences. A child can't predict or anticipate if the language used is virtually foreign to her.

Readers identify with the characters in a story in order to feel involved. We do this at any age, but very young readers or listeners have not yet learned to see the characters as imaginary. For them the actions and the people may be all too real, too close to home for comfort. Skilful authors know this and put a great deal of expertise into a seemingly simple book.

BOOKS TO SHARE ONCE AT SCHOOL

Your child's experience of the world is dramatically broadened when she starts school. She may hear friends talk of a television programe they watch and feel she must watch it too. Some of these are based on stories and books are available to go with them. They fit in with her sense of belonging to a group, and will give her practice in reading a story she already knows.

A cassette may also be available and she can listen to the tape while reading the book. Rupert Bear or Paddington may go with you in the car too. *Masters of the Universe* or *Transformers* may not be what *you* enjoy reading, but you could share books you like and offer a tape of these so that your child is 'one of the crowd' in the playground. *Thomas the Tank Engine* and *Tales of Beatrix Potter* seem popular cassettes.

COMICS?

Comic strips and books produced in this style do not seem like 'reading work' as children puzzle out the speech bubbles of, say *Tin Tin*. This may prove a way in to reading for your child. The layout and nonsense of some *Cat In The Hat* books (Dr Seuss, Collins, 1980) also appear outside mainstream books as far as new readers perceive them. Pat Hutchins' *Don't Forget the Bacon* (Penguin, 1978) has the text entirely in speech bubbles, Posy Simmonds' *Fred* is a comic strip format. They give the reader that all-knowing superiority that children love. Real comics often contain or portray questionable values but many books in this style are an excellent read. Tin Tin and Asterix have delighted children and adults alike for years.

HUMOUR

As your child grows towards 6, humour and riddles dawn on her as if for the first time in history. You will hear the same joke re-told endlessly. The coming of knock-knock jokes is inevitable and sick jokes will follow! Books of riddles are very popular. Go for paperbacks that can be carried around easily, for the child hooked on them will want to try them out on all comers. Try too a book such as Peggy Parish's *Amelia Bedelia* (World's Work, 1964) where each instruction given to Amelia is carried out literally . . . with dreadful consequences. These word jokes, puns, open up a new area for games with words as your child realizes what can be done with them. The sight of Amelia drawing the curtains and dressing the chicken has the reader roaring with laughter.

Funny poems and stories are plentiful for this age group, and you reel from *The Worst Witch* (Jill Murphy, Penguin, 1978) to *Funnybones* by Janet and Alan Ahlberg (Armada Books, 1982), with the *Ha Ha Bonk Book* ever present (Ahlberg and Ahlberg, Young Puffin Books, Penguin, 1982). Now is a good time to meet Arthur's family. Of these the funniest character is Arthur's Granny (built like a brick). She drives a car as flat as a slab of cheese, but speeds into the river with a car load of kids. This is no problem, though, for when they fear they'll drown she says 'Nonsense, climb up on me.' (*Arthur's Granny* is written by Kit Wright.)

NON-FICTION

Some readers of around 6½ like non-fiction. They like to find out from a book how to care for their puppy, or how space rockets work.

FICTION

At this stage some readers will be fluent, others more hesitant. A wide difference of ability begins to show and it is vital that slower readers do not get any sense of failure or falling behind. Choose books for them very carefully. It is very disheartening to stick on one book for ages while those around you are romping through several. This child needs a sense of achievement too. She needs to read more than a page or two to a listening adult. Together you can read a story at a sitting, share the reading and help her enjoy the whole effect of the story.

To encourage this reader, books must be especially enticing. What the children see as 'baby books' are insulting, and they are very aware of little nuances. A child might be told by another that her baby brother can read that book and he is only four. Take a fresh look and choose something which the child can manage, but which is not simplistic.

John Burningham's *Come Away From the Water Shirley* (Jonathan Cape, 1977) provides a great deal to think and talk about. *My Naughty Little Sister* by Dorothy Edwards (Magnet Books, 1982) might strike a chord. Shirley Hughes' Alfie in *Alfie Gets in First* and *Alfie Gives a Hand* (Armada Books, 1982 and 1985), is a character a six-year-old will love. *John Brown, Rose and The Midnight Cat* by Jenny Wagner and illustrated by Ron Brooks (Penguin, 1985), is an artistic, thought-provoking book. It raises issues you will want to talk about afterwards. The text is simple and easy.

Maurice Sendak's *Where the Wild Things Are* (Penguin, 1970) is not in any way babyish. In fact, to cope with it you need to be a mature six going towards seven, for it can disturb before it reassures. Easy to read and interesting enough for sixes is *Mrs Plug the Plumber* by Allan Ahlberg (Penguin, 1980). In choosing for this age group it is vital not to underestimate their curiosity, their energy and intelligence. Several fairy tales are best read now as they make demands on the readers that a four-year-old cannot supply.

POETRY

Poetry is flourishing for young children and they delight in it. Some poetry books are worth buying for your home library.

Let them meet Michael Rosen, Kit Wright, Spike Milligan, Edward Lear and A. A. Milne. Now available in the UK is the work of the American poet Shel Silverstein, *Where the Sidewalk Ends* (Jonathan Cape, 1984) and more. Read Jill Bennet's *Roger Was a Razor Fish* (Hippo Books, 1983), and the compilation *Tiny Tim* (Armada Books, 1984), verses for children that she assembled with the help of her class. Quentin Blake's *Nursery Rhyme Book* (Armada Books, 1985) introduces his wacky style which children immediately recognize. Include Michael Rosen's books, and some Roald Dahl work, West Indian poetry . . .

SONGS

For the child whose reading is developing slowly, the circularity of a tale that she already knows from the song, such as *There's a Hole in My Bucket* (William Stobbs, Oxford University Press, 1982) means that it unfolds effortlessly. Another of these is *There Was an Old Lady Who Swallowed a Fly* (Child's Play, 1975). Both are funny and cassettes are available although hardly needed if you sing the song with the child a few times.

READING SCHEMES

During a term in which I 'heard children read' from the colour-coded books on the classroom shelf, I was never once approached by a child who wanted to discuss their book. But, since taking children out of the classroom to the library for long personal choosing sessions, or book adventures, children come running up to tell me about their books. Some will stop me on the pavement outside school hours to tell me they brought the book back to change. We may even talk about books over the frozen peas in the local supermarket. There are always eager children wanting to share what they have read.

Some weak reading schemes have a controlled vocabulary and unnaturally short, contrived sentences. A series of incidents rapidly arises in an unconnected and undeveloped way, along with poor character development. This may be the diet your child will face, if the reception class she goes to does not offer children real books, or 'free choice' until they have passed through the graded stages of a scheme. If this is the case, though it happens less often nowadays, then a parent is the child's best hope for introducing a rich and varied diet of real literature.

Classrooms are markedly richer in 'real books' these days but many still colour code them, thus inferring that those children reading 'red' books are above those who 'are still on blue'. This creates a stages-type structure, which is not necessary. If enough time and attention is given to children as they choose from as wide a range as possible, they will not feel a competitive tension or take one more of the reds whether they like it or not because it is on the shelf they must finish in order to 'go up'. At home, without all this 'structure' your child can develop her *own* taste and critical sense by real free choice.

TAKING TIME TO CHOOSE

When someone is going to 'hear' a child read, the child feels that it is impolite to dither about and, in general, feels obliged to get a book and come over and read something fairly quickly. The idea seems to be that it is a waste of time for the adult (usually a parent) who is waiting to be read to, if the child potters about. Teachers frequently say, 'Quickly, choose a book and go and read to Mrs Jones.'

The choice of the book is paramount, at all ages. In the case of a beginner, the child may have a favourite and ask you to share it. You can expand the repertoire by browsing through suitable books together. Read through books yourself before reading them aloud. In the case of six- to seven-year-olds, most of whom are now reading, developing their desire to read and keeping them in the reading world are priorities. There must be a reward for reading. Making the effort and commitment deserves a good book. Finding that book may take time and patience.

This role falls naturally to the parents. We know our child well. We may be pushed for time but we have only to find the time for our own children, not for each child in a class of 28. If we have older children they can point out their favourite books to a sibling. Children as young as four feel like heroes when asked to suggest what books they think their two-year-old brother or sister might like. Always treat the child with consideration. Her taste and opinions are important. Respect her comments and notice what she likes.

The most special and personal of all books are those made for that child. Illustrations can be photos or drawings. Binding is simple with cheap plastic binders, or a local copy shop will bind your book and put on a heavy plastic cover for a low price. The book can take its place on the bookshelf along with all the others.

These books will be easy to read, especially if they are in the child's own words. They will be familiar and trusted. The author will know exactly what to expect. Anticipation and prediction are important factors. For more ideas about making up your own stories, read the section on Tall stories, page 35.

Sequencing is a vital part of telling a story. When a child selects the most important aspects of a story and arranges them in some order to make the story work, a great deal of intelligent editing is going on.

IT'S OK TO DISLIKE A BOOK

It took me many weeks to get the message across to a group of six- and seven-year-olds that 'It is OK to dislike a *particular* book.' This is distinct from disliking reading in general. How many children decide that reading is 'boring' on the strength of one book?

Very young children believe that they have to accept whatever text they are given by their teacher, librarian and even some parents. They also know that they are supposed to 'like' and respect books. When asked if they liked a book, they invariably say 'Yes' at first, only to elaborate later if asked questions about its content and what they thought might or should have happened.

When children understand that it is acceptable and will be encouraged if they have opinions, they show that they are very discerning readers. They often know what they like and they certainly know what they don't like: 'I want a book about animals', said Jessica firmly, 'but not with a sad ending.'

They need to be told that it is not impolite to be critical of a text. If they find reading boring might the text be at fault? Another selection may prove fascinating. They will need to be able to handle books and have plenty of time to choose. Rushing to the shelf to take the next reader in a series, or the only remaining orange or green colour-coded book you have not yet got through, does nothing to build up discerning readers of the future. Writing a book report is often seen as a chore, but talking about the book with someone who has read it is quite different.

If the adult has read the book, the conversation can be

illuminating. Not least because it shows the child that you value this activity enough to have read the book yourself. You can guage the child's level of perception and help with the choosing of another book because you will have some insight into her reaction.

Experienced readers become more appreciative or critical of stories and illustrations. They have a standard against which they can compare. Introducing them to authors, sequels, other books on a theme they liked, and recognizing the illustrator's style, builds the child's critical faculties and gives her an idea of the worth of her own judgement. Reading in this way is boosting her self-esteem and her individuality. She finds herself valued, thanks to her response to books.

To sum up:

- Make it clear to readers that they can express a dislike for a particular book.
- If one or two books do not prove absorbing and satisfying, there are many more. Reading is not boring; a particular text may be.
- Respect the child's opinion and taste.
- Allow as much time as necessary for choosing books.
- Read the books yourself whenever possible.
- Discuss them together. The child's response will help you to help her choose the next book.
- Note authors or illustrators she particularly likes and look for further work they have produced.
- Encourage readers to tell each other about books.
- Include non-fiction in the books you offer.
- Make personal books yourselves.

GAMES

Questions to ask

A few questions can lead to a satisfying discussion and help a child understand a book better.

Do you think these pictures fit the story well?

Is that how you imagine him to look? If not, how do you picture him in your mind?

Would you have had the story end differently? What do you think will happen now?

Why do you think he did this?

What do you think that far-away place looks like? What might he find there?

If you were writing this story would you have done it differently?

Are there any places in this story where you think the author has used just the right words to describe what is happening?

Could you make up another story about these characters? Has this ever happened to you? Can you think of another word for . . . . . . ?

Do you think she was right to do this? Why?

Did you find it exciting, did it make you want to know what was going to happen?

HOW TO HELP AT THE LIBRARY

Once at the library or bookshop we need to tread a fine line between foisting our choice onto a child who has not yet chosen, and giving too little constructive help. Of course we need to rush to the supermarket and the baby is getting fractious, but hurrying a child almost from the moment we enter the library can be a real problem for her. If someone were to say to an adult, 'Now choose quickly, I have only got ten minutes', many adults would simply say that they could not choose now and would come back another time when there was less pressure. Readers need to handle books, and browse through several before choosing.

The rows and rows of books on ever higher shelves may appear daunting to someone barely able to reach the fourth. Where is the section to start looking? Large size picture books are stored in low-level stacking boxes in most children's libraries, and there may be cushions on which to sit and examine the books. Carousels of paperbacks are not always easy for a child to deal with. Many children cannot see the titles clearly and books are stacked one behind the other on certain designs of stand. Some eight-year-olds who enjoy these books cannot reach them. You may be needed to take down a few. Be generous and hand a child several to browse through. Let her sit down and handle them.

Talking about the books the child has enjoyed and coming to know more about the authors will give a start to the hunt. Is there another by the same person? How do you look this up? Children can soon master an index or microfiche as skilfully as they master TV and video remote controls. The hunt for the number is easy, and then the child may be left to consider which, if any, of the titles will appeal.

WILL MUM APPROVE?

We all know the feeling of impatience as the child simply cannot find a book. This is often due to a feeling of conflict in the child. She feels she ought to take something at her reading level, or something that you approve of, yet she may be drawn to something simpler. Reading tastes range backward and forward in children as they do in adults. Perhaps today is the day for a western after reading *War and Peace?* A fluent reader may want to take a pop-up book, but not know what reaction this will cause in the critical adult.

What of 'trashy' books? Even these 'formula' books, churned out along the same lines, are OK if they succeed in hooking the child's interest and desire to read.

How many inveterate adult readers do you know who were hooked on *Just William*, or *The Famous Five* or *The Hardy Boys* and, the reverse of the coin, *Nancy Drew*? Formula books maybe, but loved by many. For the child who needs a comic format there is no better than *Tin Tin*, and an obsession with him seems to have worked wonders with many readers I know.

When a child saves pocket money and haunts second-hand book stalls for one more *Hardy Boys* that he hasn't read, he is laying down good reading habits. The message has been received that books equal pleasure.

If the child gets the idea that you are trying to wean her off the chosen series, she will cling ever more fiercely to it. Help by keeping an eye open for odd ones to borrow from friends or in Oxfam shops. Your help in finding the book she wants will be valued, and then, if you come up with other suggestions they will be seriously considered, for you have not spurned her taste.

What they enjoy

As a generalization, three- to four-year-olds enjoy repetition and familiarity. Stories with warm secure endings, the problem solved and 'all wrapped up'.

A four-year-old will adore flap books and pop-ups along with fascinating ABCs, poetry rhymes and chants.

Fives want action: a good story line, realism and fantasy. They will enjoy prose but be discovering poetry too.

Sixes and sevens, while still wanting stories with action, will be keen on humour. Riddles and jokes are their currency. At seven a reader can distinguish better between the real world and fantasy.

For this reason many parents prefer to keep the more frightening fairy-tales until now.

Readers range back and forth in their reading taste, expanding their range while building confidence.

LET'S NOT ARGUE ABOUT BOOKS

I have sat in children's libraries for many hours compiling lists of books that are favourites. I can't help overhearing some of the conversations around me. The most upsetting are those in which a child firmly clutches a book to her chest while the adult tries to explain that it is too hard or too something.

If your child has chosen a book that you feel may be too difficult for her to read or understand, simply take it home along with the others, and read it together. If you read it to each other you can help cross any hurdles. It is remarkable how a child's reading skill seems to improve to meet a book she is especially interested in.

In silent reading, the reader does not necessarily understand or even fully read every word, but she gets the gist of the meaning and the story holds her imagination. Your child can feel free to ask for your help with a book when she needs it. She may, however, get the general meaning from a page which seems too difficult for her, because she has an interest in this subject and can effectively guess or supply the words she needs.

- If someone else takes your child to the library – Gran, or another carer – make your views on book choosing very clear. I have heard heated arguments between nannies and children about the suitability of books. The carer is worried that the parents will look at the book at home and wonder why she allowed that unsuitable choice. Carers may not be well equipped to handle this unless you indicate your ideas.
- As your child grows as a reader, her confidence will increase and she will become more aware of the wider world of books.

With more background knowledge of the library and what it holds, the whole procedure will become easier.

Use the time the child spends browsing to look through lists the library has prepared for this age group. You might read through magazines with reviews of children's books (there is a list of these on page 148).

Try to make choosing a happy, relaxed event with no tension, argument or 'Hurry up'. If she sees you engrossed in reading yourself, or aloud to another child, she won't feel that you are tensely waiting for her to choose.

7

Success Begins at Home

RESEARCH INTO THE ROLE OF PARENTS

In 1964, J. W. B. Douglas' study entitled 'The home and the school: A study of ability and attainment in the primary school' was published. In this research, 4,000 children were studied at 8 years old and then again at 11. The information that was gathered on how well they were doing at school was then looked at to see how it related to various home factors and the level of interest the parents showed in their child's schooling. Clear social class differences were found in reading success and Douglas argued that this gap widened during the period of the study. However, within each social class, the level of the parents' interest (as judged by the schools) was shown to be very strongly related to the child's attainment: 'The child's capacity to do well at his work in school is, to a certain degree, dependent on the encouragement he gets from his parents.'

The Plowden report in 1967 reflected the theory that parental concern and attitudes towards schools and education are major factors in predicting the child's success at school. This report found too that the parents' attitudes were only partly explained by their material circumstance and education.

In 1978, J. Sallis looked at the schools' lack of enthusiasm for forging genuine links with parents. She noted that, despite the fact that parents were continually being told of their vital contribution to their child's success, they were not being given a genuine role to play (*Parents and School,* BBC Publications, 1978). J. Freeman, in *In and Out of School* (Methuen, 1975), offered some reasons for the schools' seeming reluctance to do this: '. . . schools that fear that by opening the door a crack, the status of the teacher will drop, can have very little faith in their own expertise, and it is likely that this attitude will be apparent in greater rigidity and control in the school system.'

Eric Midwinter, in *Education for Sale* (Allen & Unwin, 1977) put paid to the myth of 'parental apathy' and reminded us that the child is not taught solely in school hours.

By the early seventies, schools began to pay lip service to the idea of parental involvement, but not all that much was happening to make it workable. The Taylor report looked at the influence parents might have in schools. *A New Partnership for Schools* (DES, 1977) recommended that parents be represented on governing bodies along with staff and LEA representatives. Parents were to be involved in their child's progress and welfare and each parent should receive a booklet stating the outlook and aims of the school. The many recommendations of this report are having far-reaching effects on the school system and many more were incorporated into the 1980 Education Act.

The influence of home

A clear indication of how much the home influences children in their success at school emerged from the national child development study of children from birth to seven carried out by J. and E. Newsom in 1977 (*Perspectives on School at Seven Years Old*, Allen & Unwin, 1977). The study found evidence of the relationship between social class and reading attainment. However, they found that the majority of working-class parents were trying to help their children with reading. These parents understood that they played an important part in their child's education but the willingness to help was '. . . too often mis-channelled for lack of advice, encouragement and appreciation . . .' They pointed out that schools were failing in their educative role and wasting the most valuable resource they have. They wrote, 'A revolution in literacy could be sparked off and fuelled by parents and teachers in determined co-operation'.

Already J. Hewison had found in a series of studies in 1976 that the factor in the home background which most strongly affected the child's reading progress was whether or not the mother regularly heard the child read. There were other factors too, of course, which affected the child's reading achievement, among them the attitudes of parents towards learning, a high IQ, and parents who were themselves keen readers.

School and home as partners

The idea of helping parents from all walks of life and educational backgrounds to help their children was put into action when the Haringey project was set up. Research was carried out from 1976 until 1978 and there were also follow-up checks. The report was published in 1982 and looked at the question of whether or not significant gains could be achieved when all parents were involved in a reading project.

Some of the families in this area did not have English as a mother tongue. The study was looking at children's progress based on home help irrespective of social class or home language. Many results were encouraging. Parents with very little education themselves were keen to collaborate and proved effective. Support was high and both teachers and parents were enthusiastic. Parents were also visited at home and welcomed advice.

Interestingly, despite many predictions to the contrary, there was negligible damage or loss to the books sent home. The gains achieved by the group of children receiving help at home in this project were measured against those gains made by children in small withdrawal groups who received help from a remedial teacher four times a week, and the gains made by control groups. (There can be no totally accurate accounting, for parents in other groups may be helping their child at home in any case.)

A great deal of publicity was given to the finding that *all* children, irrespective of social class or ethnic background, could achieve better results in reading if they are heard regularly at home. Both parents and teachers found this rewarding. The children clearly found encouragement and support.

Other projects have been set up to look closely at the parental contribution to reading. Among them were The Belfield Reading Project in Rochdale and PACT (Parents Children and Teachers) in Hackney. Reading projects were set up and monitored in West Glamorgan and in Dorset and there have been projects in Hackney, Newham and Berkshire. Parents are joining with teachers to form a partnership to help children with reading. Real and imaginary signs saying 'No parents beyond this point' have disappeared.

Parents have a unique concern for their child, no matter where they are. This natural concern can be channelled into a productive, exciting co-operation between school and home, supporting the child through secure partnership.

Details of the many reports and surveys along with resource material are listed in a booklet entitled *Involving Parents in the Teaching of Reading – Some key sources* (University of Sheffield).

SCHOOL JARGON

Integrated day

This is the opposite of a strictly timetabled day. The children work at their own pace to accomplish a series of activities that the teacher has planned. The order and completion time of these varies according to the child. A child who is absorbed in writing will not suddenly have to stop in order to do number work. The child who cannot get started sometimes floats along doing very little.

Vertical or family grouping

When a class is vertically grouped the pupils are not all the same age. The young ones learn from the older ones, and the older children practise what they have learned. This system can create a caring classroom, into which a beginner is easily absorbed and taken care of. Naturally there are only a few beginners at any one time.

Reception class

The first class in the infant school.

Setting

Children of similar abilities are taught together in sets or groups.

The hidden curriculum

The school's standards, policies, discipline and attitudes.

Team teaching

This is a form of job share, when more than one teacher shares the teaching of a class.

Cuisenaire rods

A system of counting and measuring using coloured rods representing different values.

Things you may like to ask about the school

- Special diets and religious requirements.
- Parent involvement - how welcome are parents? Do they help in school? How? Do they raise funds? Do they go on outings, share expertise?
- Do I need an appointment or can I talk to you at any time?
- How do you let me know about my child's progress or problems?
- What do you do about bullying?

You may have to try to assess for yourself the policy on racism or sexism from what you see in and around the school. This is true also of the school's attitude to parents. Some schools may have a stated policy of involving the parents, who have been told that they are welcome any time. In practice, however, parents might have to congregate at the gate to wait for their children. Going in to look for the teacher might be the exception. It might have been subtly made clear that teachers are very busy and are not simply hanging around for parents to collar them for a little chat.

Parents feel that if they must make an appointment or send in a letter, then the matter must be fairly important. The odd casual question does not seem to warrant this, so little worries may build up. In schools where the parents are encouraged to come to the classroom or the library to collect the children, there is ample opportunity for a *brief* word. This can be useful to the teacher who might want to tell you something. Collecting a child from the school library allows you to read quietly to a younger brother or sister while waiting. Fetching from the classroom allows your child to show you what he made today. This means that you know how he is doing and do not need to ask.

On the subject of reading, certain jargon phrases can make parents feel outsiders.

- **The real book approach** or **free choice.** The school teaches children to read using books by authors and illustrators rather than reading schemes produced by publishers with a controlled vocabulary as a teaching device. The children are exposed to a wide range of appropriate books, they do not go up stages or levels or colours, but read a variety of books like any reader.

- **Phonics.** A method of learning to read by sounding out the letters and blending them to make the word. English often confounds the rules.

- **Flash cards** and **Look and say.** The child learns to read by recognizing words.

- **Colour coding** is a system of grading books by marking those of a similar level with the same colour. Children are expected to read the 'red' books until permitted to go up to 'black'.

- **PACT** is one of several schemes involving parents in their child's reading. Children bring home books to read with their parents and there is dialogue between school and home. Parents, children and teachers work together.

- **Language experience** describes a method of using the child's spoken words, writing them down and reading them back. A variety of ways exist to use the child's language ability to broaden his reading and writing.

- **Breakthrough to literacy** is a popular method using sentence-making kits that allow the child to make sentences by putting words together easily. The child does not have to write well to express himself. Reading and writing develop from this.

Further Reading and Resources
· · · · ·

THE ROLE OF PARENTS

If you wish to read further about the role of parents in the teaching process, this list may be helpful.

Hannon, P., Long, R., Weinberger, J., and Whitehurst, L., *Involving Parents in the Teaching of Reading* - Some key sources. (USDE papers in education, 1985, available from the University of Sheffield)

Children and Their Primary Schools (The Plowden Report) (DES, 1967, available from HMSO)

A Language for Life (The Bullock Report) (DES, 1975, available from HMSO)

A New Partnership for Our Schools (The Taylor report) (DES, 1977, available from HMSO)

Freeman, J., *In and Out of Schools* (Methuen, 1976)

Griffiths, A., and Hamilton, D., Parent Teacher Child Alliance, *Working Together in Children's Learning* (Methuen, 1984) and *Learning at Home* (Methuen, 1987)

Goodacre, E., *Reading Research Review* (University of Reading, 1985)

Hewison, J., and Tizard, S., 'Parental Involvement and Reading Attainment', British Journal of Educational Psychology, Vol. 50, pages 209-15, 1980

ILEA Pitfield Project, 'Home-School Reading Partnerships in Hackney' (Inner London Education Authority, 1984)

Jackson A., and Hannon, P., 'The Belfield Reading Project' (Rochdale, Belfield Community Council, 1981)

Midwinter, E., *Education For Sale* (Allen & Unwin, 1977)

Newson, J., and Newson, E., *Perspectives on School at Seven Years Old* (Allen & Unwin, 1977)

Sallis, J., *Parents and School* (BBC Publications, 1978)

Schofield, V., *Haringey Reading Project* (final report to DES, 1979)

Southgate, V., *Extending Beginning Reading* (Heinemann, 1981)

Tizard, B., and Hughes, M., *Young Children Learning* (Fontana, 1984)

Tizard, J., Schofield, W. N., and Hewison, J., 'Collaboration Between Teachers and Parents in Assisting Children's Reading', British Journal of Educational Psychology, Vol. 52, pages 1-15, 1982

Topping, K., and Wolfendale, S., (eds), *Parental Involvement in Children's Reading* (Croom Helm, 1985)

Waterland, L., *Read With Me* (Thimble Press, 1985)

Wilby, P., 'The Belfield Experiment', *The Sunday Times*, 29 March, 1981

HOW TO FIND A GOOD READ

Where to find out about books for children. Your local library is always a good source of books and information.

Butler, D., *Five to Eight* and *Babies Need Books* (Bodley Head, 1986/Penguin, 1982)

Teenager to Young Adult (School Library Association)

Suggests reading for ethnic minority pupils and ways of coping with racial prejudice. It covers humour, school life, the world of work, sport and competition, heroines, ethnic minorities, fantasy, science fiction, ghost stories and legends, adventure, thrillers, political and historical fiction and family relationships.

Bennett, J., *Learning to Read With Picture Books* (Thimble Press, 1985)

Bradman, T., *I Need a Book* (Thorsons, 1986)

Graham, J., and Plackett, E., *Developing Readers* - Books to encourage children and young people to read, (School Library Association, 1987)

Lapage, G., *101 Good Read Alouds for 5-11 Year Olds* (Reading and Language Information Centre, University of Reading School of Education, 1987)

Morris, H., *Where's That Poem?* (Basil Blackwell, 1985)

Finding a poem about Samson or sardines? Where-to-find-it references in this fascinating directory.

Reading for Enjoyment series (Baker Book Services 0-6, 7-11, 12-15, 16 and up)

Trelease, J., *The Read Aloud Handbook* (Penguin, 1984)

Children's Books for a Multicultural Society 0-7 and 8-12 (Published by the School Bookshop Association, 6 Brightfield Road, Lee, London SE12 8QF)

Other Languages

Enquire at your local library about Luzac story-tellers – a series in a wide range of languages.

Ingham Yates is a dual language list and to find out more, write to them c/o Baker Book Services, 10/11 Manfield Park, Guildford Road, Cranleigh, Surrey GU6 8NU

Library books

Books you may want to consult occasionally in the library are:
Reading About Children's Books, Lance Salway (National Book League, 1986)
An introductory guide to books about children's literature.
Who's Who in Children's Books, Fisher, M., (Weidenfeld and Nicholson, 1975)

JOURNALS

UK

Bookmark
News of Children's Literature worldwide, available from the English Department, Heriott Watt University, Holyrood Campus, Holyrood Road, Edinburgh EH8 8AG

Bookquest
Selections and reviews by staff, students and teachers, available from The Education Department, University of Sussex, Falmer, Brighton, East Sussex BN1 9RG

Books for Keeps
Bi-monthly magazine for teachers and librarians, contains reviews, features, news about TV and film. Mainly paperbacks. Produces good multicultural lists and background information. Available from 6 Brightfield Road, Lee, London SE12 8QF or ask in your local library.

Books For Your Children
Three issues per year, intended for parents. Available from 34 Harborne Road, Edgbaston, Birmingham B15 3AA

Further Reading and Resources

British Book News, Children's Books
Reviews and articles about children's literature available from Children's Books, The British Council, 65 Davies Street, London W1V 2AA

Child Education
Infant School emphasis, with reviews and project ideas, available from Scholastic Publications, Villiers House, Clarendon Avenue, Leamington Spa, Warwickshire CV32 5PR

The Children's Book Foundation
Free Parent Packs – specify age of child – available from Book House, 44 East Hill, London SW18 2QZ

Children's Books in Scotland
Produced by the Committee for Children's Books in Scotland and available from The Book Trust in Scotland

Children's Review of Books

Dragon's Tale
Articles and reviews on children's books in Wales, available from the Welsh Books Council, Castell Brychan, Heol-y-Bryn, Aberystwyth, Dyfed SY23 2JB, Wales

The Egg!
Magazine for children from 4 to 8 years, including stories, articles, reviews and competitions. Available from The Junior Puffin Club, Penguin Books, Bath Road, Harmondsworth, Middlesex UB7 0DA

Good Book Guide
Contains a children's book section. Subscription includes *The Good Book Guide to Children's Books*. Available from P.O. Box 400, 101 Avro House, Havelock Terrace, London SW8 4AU

Institute of Education
Gives general information. University of London, 20 Bedford Way, London WC1N 0AL

The Junior Bookshelf
A British review of books available from Marsh Hall, Thurstonland, Huddersfield HD4 6XB

Junior Education

Book information and project ideas available from Scholastic Publications Limited, Villiers House, Clarendon Avenue, Leamington Spa, Warwickshire CV32 5PR

Puffin Post

A magazine for children from 8 to 14 contains stories, articles, reviews and competitions. Available from The Puffin Club, Penguin Books Limited, Bath Road, Harmondsworth, Middlesex UB7 0DA

The School Librarian

Indexed reviews plus articles of interest to school librarians. Available from the School Library Association, 83 Warwick St, Oxford OX4 1SZ

Signal

Independent articles on all aspects of children's books. Available from Nancy Chambers, Thimble Press, Lockwood, Station Road, South Woodchester, Stroud, Gloucestershire GL5 5EQ

The Times Educational Supplement

Weekly signed reviews by regular contributors

Newspaper review pages – especially before Christmas. Look too in magazines for parents and *Good Housekeeping,* a magazine which occasionally runs special features.

Australia

Reading Time

The journal of the Children's Book Council of Australia, available from P.O. Box 62, Turvey Park, NSW 2650.

Review

A school libraries journal, available from School Libraries Branch, P.O. Box 1152, GPO Adelaide 5001.

New Zealand

Booknotes

This gives news of children's literature in New Zealand, and is available from the New Zealand Book Council, P.O. Box 11377, Wellington Book House, Boulcott St, Wellington, New Zealand (six per annum).

Children's Literature Association Yearbook
This is available from the Children's Literature Association of New Zealand,
  P.O. Box 36036, Northcote, Auckland 9.

Canada

Canadian Children's Literature
This is available from the Canadian Children's Literature Association, P.O. Box
  335, Guelph, Ontario N1H 6K5.

Children's Book News
This is available from the Children's Book Centre, 5th Floor, 229 College St,
  Toronto, Ontario M5T 1KA.

ASSOCIATIONS

Federation of Children's Book Groups is a national body fostering children's
  book groups in cities, towns and villages.
School Bookshop Association and their journal *School Bookshop News* are of
  interest. They have an interest in Community publishing and Multi-ethnic
  projects.

Appendix: The Story of Reading

Child knows what a book is.

Which way up it goes, which is front/back.

Turns pages.

Enjoys stories and pictures.

Pretends to read.

Looks at books alone right way up.

Turns pages for you as you read.

Points to pictures and spots detail.

Reading is a time for loving and talking and sharing the book.

Recites stories from memory.

Follows adult reading known text.

Has favourites.

Joins in repetition.

Willing and eager to 'read'.

'Reads' know text accurate

Finger points and follows reading.

Knows letters and sounds.

Recognizes ke words and notices some of them out of context.

Attempts to read text.

Aware of prin

Brings books to adult to share.

Uses context, syntax, sound clues, pictures and memory to recall known text.

Can discuss story and understand it.

Personal vocabulary growing.

Making complex sentences.

Guesses unknown text.

Reading some public print.

Makes own books.

Begins to read back own words written out by adult.

Predicts stories and events.

Recognizes key words in a text.

Reading some public print.

Reads known text independently.

Gaining skill and confidence to tackle unknown words.

Self-corrects from meaning if you ask about this.

Predicting and scanning ahead.

Begins to try unknown text with adult support.

Reads with intelligence and expression, no longer one word at a time. Reads for fun. Reads to self.

Chooses books confidently.

Able to tackle unknown text alone.

Writes own sentences and reads them back.

Index
. . . . .